Where Credit is Due

Take Some Credit 25
Students Fall Easily into the Credit Trap 36
A Holiday Credit Saver 49
How the Government Sees It 82
Rating our Plastic Pals. 88
FAQ: Using Credit Wisely 89
An A+ or and F? 90
FAQ: 10 Ways to Protect Your Credit Cards 94

Protecting Yourself and Others

Car Insurance? Better Start Saving Now 2
FAQ: Car Insurance 4
FAQ: Tenant Insurance 17
Car Collision Musts 62
FAQ: Employment Insurance 65
FAQ: Insurance 86

To Market, To Market

Ask Kris: Calling All Consumers 6
The Big Bucks Business Behind Rock Concerts 20
Bartering. 26
Digital Deflation 30
Glitch Cartoon 36
For Better or For Worse cartoon 51
Tips for Smart Catalogue Shopping 54
You've Got Clout 56
Reboot Your Home Office 59
How Not to Buy a Lemon 61
Walking Down the Aisles 63
Ziggy Cartoon 65
Low-Impact Living 70
Does Buying Green Mean Paying More? 71
Sustainable Development 71
It Came From Outer Scalp 74
What Does It Say On the Label? 77
Health Tip: Spotting Health Fraud 78
Complaining the Write Way 87
Special Offers? 91

Venturing Out

Leaving Home. 14
Renting Without Confusion 16
Nothing Stays the Same Forever 25
Energy$aver Checklist. 33
Leaving the Nest 34
Your In-Home Water Audit 37
Rules of the Road When Setting Up 38
Power Shopping 40
Home Again 42
Know Where Your Power Goes 60
New Roommate? Ask Questions 66
Peanuts cartoon 67
How to Choose, Keep, or Lose a Roommate. 68
10 Tips for Living On Your Own 69
One Loony Will... 72
B.C. cartoon. 78

Credits 97

Author
Judith Campbell

Publisher
Rob Greenaway

Editor
Julia Lee

Production Manager
Gail de Acevedo

Art Director
Alex Li

Design
Anne Goodes

Cover photograph
Birgitte Nielsen

Illustrations
Scot Ritchie   Teco Guerreiro Rodrigues   Kevin Cheng
Paul McCusker   Dave Whamond

Inside Photographs
Dick Hemmingway

Permissions
Angelika Baur
Karen Taylor

Canadian Cataloguing in Publication Data

Campbell, Judith, date
Venturing Out
(Lifechoices)
ISBN: 0-13-244278-7

1. Life skills. I. Title. II. Series.

HQ2037.C35 1997   646.7   C96-932402-2

LIFECHOICES: Student Resources
Relationships: 0-13-242173-9
Healthy and Well: 0-13-244195-0
Venturing Out: 0-13-244278-7
Careers: 0-13-244211-6

LIFECHOICES: Teacher Resources
Relationships: 0-13-242181-X
Healthy and Well: 0-13-244203-5
Venturing Out: 0-13-244286-8
Careers: 0-13-244252-3

Many thanks to Wade Cummings and Merit Insurance for their help.
Every reasonable effort has been made to find copyright holders
for material contained in this book. The publishers would be
pleased to have any errors or omissions brought to their attention.

Printed and bound in Canada

2 3 4 5 TCP 07 06 05 04

Car Insurance? Better Start Saving Now

T hinking of buying a car? Start saving now for car insurance - it's very expensive. If you are between 16 and 21 years old, you may pay about three times as much as a 25-year-old with a clean driving record. You may also be surprised to learn that it makes very little difference whether you are driving the newest sports car or the oldest truck - the rates are almost the same.

Financially-smart teenagers find any other way to get around for as long as they can - bus, bike or walking - to save the high costs of being a young car owner.

These high insurance rates probably don't seem fair but they are based on the history and records kept by insurance companies. Teenagers are more likely to have a heavy foot on the gas, run the odd red light, and, in general, lack driving experience, a proven driving record and road smarts.

What about if you sometimes use your parents' car? If you are an occasional user of your parents' car, you can be added to your parents' car insurance coverage, if your parents are willing, as an *occasional operator*. This is much cheaper than owning your own car, even if you are contributing to fuel and upkeep costs. (And filling the tank after you use the family car is a good idea anytime, as is contributing to your parents' increased insurance rates.) Having four or five years of clear driving as an occasional operator can also make it easier for you to get car insurance, if and when you finally buy your own vehicle. So, the best advice for

"Having four or five years of clear driving as an occasional operator can make it easier for you to get car insurance, if and when you finally buy your own vehicle."

now - find other ways to get around, save your money, and be an "occasional operator" for a few years.

However, if you are a teenager and a car owner, or you are planning to

be, there are some important thing you need to know. One thing you ca do that may help, and certainly can hurt, is taking a driver's trainin course. While the cost of the cours

n be a couple of hundred dollars or
more, the insurance savings for some-
ne who has taken the course may be
bout the same amount of money.
nd you get the benefit of having a
river's course on your record.

What exactly is car insurance?

Insurance is a protection you pur-
hase so that, when you suffer a fi-
ancial loss, it is paid by the insurance
ompany. The amount you pay to the
nsurance company is called a *premium*. Your premium, in combination
ith thousands of other drivers' pre-
iums, forms a pool of money so that
 you need coverage (having your
ills paid), the insurance company will
rovide that coverage and pay those
ills. In the case of car insurance, it
rotects you from the financial bur-
en you would face on your own, if
ou were involved in a car accident.
ou must have car insurance by law
ecause the pay-outs can be so high
at you can be financially destroyed,
ow and in the future, by even a rel-
tively small accident.

Car insurance is not the same in
ll provinces so it is important for you
 investigate the specifics of the car
nsurance required in your province.
lowever, you are required by law to
uy some form of car insurance if you
wn a vehicle and drive it on public
oads in Canada. You have coverage
hen you sign up with an insurance
ompany, agent, or broker. All of the
overage is written into your policy.

Car insurance has several compo-
ents. One piece is *Liability* (often
alled Third Party Liability) insur-
nce. If you injure or kill another per-
on or damage another person's car,
ou need to have enough liability in-
urance to cover the claim or claims
gainst you. Any amount claimed
gainst you above your level of cov-
rage, you will have to pay yourself.
hese amounts can be huge, hun-
reds of thousands of dollars, so hav-
ng enough liability coverage is really
mportant.

Accident Benefits insurance is com-
pulsory almost everywhere in Canada.
It covers you, your passengers, and
pedestrians if they are injured or killed
in an automobile accident.

Uninsured automobile insurance is
included with Accidents Benefits insurance in most places in Canada. This
means that you will be covered if you
are hurt or killed by someone who
does not have auto insurance.

Collision insurance covers damage to your car caused by collision
with another car, object, or upset.
Comprehensive insurance covers your
car against these hazards and other
hazards as well. *All perils* insurance
combines Collision and Comprehensive
coverages and may include theft and
glass. *Specified perils* covers your car

against loss or damage due to fire,
theft, lightning, windstorm, hail,
earthquake, explosion, riot, falling air-
craft, rising water, or an accident to a
vehicle or boat on which your car is
being transported. The best action you
can take is to work with your insurance agent to come up with the best
combination of auto insurance for you,
your situation, and your automobile.

You must have insurance; you can
be charged for failing to have it. Your
"pink slip", which must be current
and kept in your car at all times, is
the Canada-Interprovince Motor
Vehicle Liability Insurance Card and
it must be produced when demanded
by police. And it should go without
saying that you also need a valid driver's licence!

"You are required by law to buy some form of car insurance if you own a vehicle and drive it on public roads in Canada"

FAQ Car Insurance

◆ The laws and regulations about auto insurance vary from one province to another. For example, getting your driver's licence may be inexpensive in your province but the car insurance premiums may be really costly. Or it may cost you a lot for a driver's licence but the insurance premiums may be lower, Or everything might be really expensive!

◆ Remember to include your car insurance premiums in your budget. You can pay annually, quarterly (every three months) or every month. And, in some areas of Canada, you can have the payments directly paid from your bank account.

◆ Car insurance does not cover normal wear-and-tear or mechanical breakdown of your car. Those are other items which have to be built into your budget.

◆ The cost of insurance can be affected by several things, like your driving record, the number of tickets you have had, and the number of claims you have made in the past.

◆ A **deductible** is the amount you have agreed to pay before your insurance kicks in. It is not the premium which must be paid as agreed. A deductible is paid when there is an accident. Say you have Collision insurance with a deductible of $250. That means that you must pay $250 of any repair bill before your insurance company kicks in and pays the rest. Or you might have a deductible of $500 before the insurance company pays. Why have a higher deductible then if it is just more money out of your own pocket? Because the premium you pay for the $250 deductible will be higher than the premium you will pay for a $500 deductible.

◆ The deductible can apply, even if the accident is not your fault. However, your insurance company will attempt to recover your deductible from the other person's insurance company.

◆ If you have an accident, you need to call your insurance company as soon as you can (not from the scene of the accident - calling an ambulance and the police is more important if there are injuries and a lot of damage).

◆ When you contact your insurance company, an **adjuster** for the company will determine what coverage you have and what will be paid. If you are claiming against someone else in the accident, you should also contact their insurance company as soon as you can. That's why it is important in an accident to get the other driver's name, pink card number, and name of insurance company.

◆ If you are found guilty of charges such as impaired driving, your insurance company is likely to decline to insure you in the future - they will not sell insurance to you. If there is a company that will sell insurance to you, it will cost you about 50% more.

◆ Know that insurance companies talk to each other - they are not easily fooled.

◆ You can damage your insurance rating with any moving violation (speeding, running a red light, driving in a bus lane are just a few). A fourth violation will raise your insurance premiums another 25% and all the violations will stay on your record for several years.

◆ And, as you already know, NEVER drive impaired by alcohol or any other drugs; never use a car phone unless you are parked or the phone is a hands-free model with a speaker in the visor; never drive an unsafe vehicle (be particularly sure that the brakes are in good working order); never drive without a valid license and insurance coverage. ALWAYS wear your seat belt; and always signal before changing lanes or direction. It pays to be a safe driver!

The Habit of
Spending

We all look at and use money differently.
How do you handle the stuff?

If I had $100 given to me, I would _____

I would put off paying a loan or a bill if _____

When it comes to money, I would say I am _____

I like to spend money on _____

When I am feeling really good about something, I _____

When I am feeling really down about something, I _____

When I am really bored, I _____

I save money by _____

If I don't have enough money for something I really want, I _____

I put off buying something if _____

The best buy I ever made is _____

It was a great buy because _____

The worst buy I ever made is _____

It was the worst buy because _____

I return things when _____

Compared to my friends, I would say my spending is _____

I spend too much money on _____

I borrow money from _____

I borrow money for _____

Ask Kris

Calling All Consumers

Q: Yesterday dinner-time I got this weird phone call. Some woman told me she'd send me some cool software for free, on trial, and then after 3 weeks I could buy it at a really good price if I wanted to. When I said Fine, send it, she asked for my credit card number. She said they need numbers for all their "Canadian customers". Was she legit?

A: Who knows, but it certainly sounds like a scam to me. Whenever anyone calls you, saying you can get something for free, they shouldn't need any money. In fact, you should never go for a deal over the phone unless you made the phone call yourself. Most important of all, never give out a credit card number (yours or anyone else's) over the phone unless you chose to call the company in the first place. There are all kinds of different phone frauds. The most common is "Congratulations, you have won our grand prize" - you just have to buy something else first, or pay some tax or other, to get the prize.

Don't believe them - they're scams.

Project Phonebusters (a national task force made up of many legal and financial institutions, including the Mounties) gives the following advice:

Don't believe that everyone calling with an exciting promotion or investment opportunity is trustworthy, especially if you do not know them or their company.

Don't be fooled by a promise of a valuable prize in return for a low cost purchase.

Don't disclose information about your bank account or credit card, not even a credit card expiry date.

Don't be pressured to send money to take advantage of a "deal".

Don't be afraid to hang up the phone.

Don't purchase or invest without carefully checking the product, the investment and the company. Don't be afraid to request further documentation from the caller so you can verify the validity of his or her company.

Hang up the phone if you are contacted by someone who promises you great prizes, but you are required to send money in advance for shipping,

handling, taxes, etc., or you must pur chase a product to qualify.

Luckily, as Canadians get mor savvy about this kind of thing, the in cidence of phone scams is decreasing but Internet scams are increasing and a lot of people are still getting burne for a lot of money. Don't be one o them!

....

Q: I keep seeing ads for free cellula phones and the other day at th mall, there was a booth where yo could sign up and get a free phone Several people at school have cel phones. Did they get them for free Should I get one?

A: The use of a cellular phone has tw costs - the purchase of the telephon and the monthly cost of the servic that gives you the use of the phone Without the service, the cell phon won't work (just like getting a car fo free and not having the gasoline yo pay for on a regular basis).

"Signing up" means signing a con

Dan Brawner/Stock Illustration Source

"Do some comparison shopping by checking out the prices of the service you want at several different companies."

tract with the company that will provide you with the connection service. Usually this is a carrier in your area; if you use your cell phone in other than local areas, you will pay for "roaming", which is often more expensive. While the advertising indicates that the cell phone is free, the actual cost of the phone is calculated into the costs of providing the service. Usually there is a monthly charge, like regular telephone service, but there is a confusing number of payment plans.

The plans offered by some companies have a set monthly fee for a certain number of minutes and then charge an extra fee per minute for every minute after that. Some companies offer a special minute rate for weekends and evenings and charge a higher fee for the "peak periods" of use, usually during business hours

when most people use them.

If you want a cell phone, do some comparison shopping by checking out the prices of the service you want at several different companies. Choose the company that offers the lowest monthly fee which meets your needs. For example, if most of your calls will be in the evening, look for low rates for that period of time. Whatever the price, figure out whether you can build this extra monthly cost into your budget. And remember, you are signing a contract, just like any other contract, and you are obligated to meet the terms which are written in that contract.

There are advantages and disadvantages of having a cellular phone. It is a good thing to have for emergencies - if you drive at night and in poor weather. But a cell phone can be an expensive investment.

Q: We have just moved into an apartment and there seems to be a lot of choices to make. The TV commercials about long distance phone rates just confuse me. How do I choose a long distance carrier?

A: Choosing a long distance carrier can be really confusing because there is fierce competition between companies to get your long distance dollars.

The first step to making this decision is to take a look at your past telephone bills - three or four months' worth. Look at the calls you have made on your family's telephone if you have been living at home until now. Who do you call long distance? How often do you call? How long are the calls? If this move takes you away from family and friends, also consider these questions.

The next step is to comparison shop for the long distance carrier and a plan which best meets your needs. If a carrier offers good prices during the day but that isn't when you will be making calls, then it might not be the right carrier for you. If a carrier offers good evening and weekend rates for calls in your province but most of your calls will be to another province or country, this may not be your best choice for a carrier.

Your big consideration should be price. Choosing a plan is important; otherwise, you will be paying the highest long distance rates the carrier has. So, choose a carrier with plans that are best for you and then sign up for a plan.

Once you have your new plan in place, check each month to see that the bill is from the same company you have chosen. If it isn't, and if you have not agreed to switch companies, then you have been "slammed"— switched from one company to another without your permission. Often, the new company charges you basic rates which can be higher than you were paying with the company you first chose. Phone your original company and complain. Ask them to reinstate you with no charge. Like I said before, the competition between phone companies is fierce!

Being Flexible

Not all plans go exactly as they are laid out. Being flexible can help you to reach a goal when the original plan is just not working. Here are some guidelines:

1. Recognize that a plan is blocked in some way.

2. Figure out what that block or obstacle is.

3. Acknowledge that the goal is still important, reasonable and worth the effort.

4. Find one or more ways around the obstacle.

5. Change the plan so that the path to the goal becomes open again.

6. Stick to it: persevere along the new path to the goal.

FAQ Getting the paperwork done

Paper, paper, paper. There are some important pieces of paper that you must be able to get your hands on. What papers do you need?

- a birth certificate
- citizenship papers
- immigration papers
- driver's licence
- Treaty card
- passport

- student number
- Social Insurance Number (SIN) card
- copies of insurance policies
- provincial health insurance card
- a list of any investments and valuable items
- transcripts from educational institutions, including high school

"Savings? Who has savings? I barely make it from one pay cheque to another." —Trishia

"I have a bank account. I would put money in it if I had any left over. But by the time I do all I have do and buy all the stuff I need, there's never any money left." —Anu

"I have a savings account. My grandparents send me cheques for my birthday and Christmas and they always go directly into the bank." —Cayce

"Sometimes I can save. It depends on how much work I get. Some weeks are really good but other times, I get zero hours so I can barely pay my expenses." —Krista

"Save for emergencies? I'm not going to have any emergencies. I mean, what kind of emergencies could an eighteen-year-old have? —Travis

"I don't have my own bank account. Part of my pay cheque goes to my parents. The rest I use to buy some of my clothes and other little stuff." —Katie

"Well, I guess I could say I save but it's only for two months a year. Then it's back to school and I don't have time to work. For the next ten months I am just withdrawing money to pay rent and tuition. Some summers I work two jobs and do extra weekend hours. —Ryan

$avings
Getting Beyond the Penny Jar

E verybody has had some experience with money—a piggy bank, a paper route, a babysitting job. And as a kid, you may have had a bank account, maybe saving for a bicycle, hockey equipment, computer game, buying souvenirs on a family vacation or for further education. These are all good practices—and kids learn a lot about saving habits in their families and for themselves. But as you move forward you need to have some strong saving skills to succeed.

That's because all the talk you have heard and all the things you have read about short-term and long-term financial goals is really about saving money: saving for short-term goals; for irregular annual expenses like car insurance; saving to buy things; saving for longer term experiences, like university, technical school, or a vacation; saving for emergencies; and saving to establish a credit rating.

If you haven't been saving up to now, get with it. Start saving while you're still living at home. Chances are that your expenses while living at home are low, even if you are paying rent.

Saving from an early age can pro-vide you with some amazing results.

The first step is to "pay yourself first". That means taking a part of your income and banking it immediately. You need a cushion for emergencies and for short-term goals—a new tire, a winter coat—you get the idea. You also need a savings account for longer term goals like university or training after high school or setting up a business.

The major skill here is self-discipline. You need to get into the habit of saving something—whatever the amount—on a regular basis.

Tips on Saving Money

☐ Look through flyers before going out shopping. Phone around. Shop around.

☐ If you have the storage space, buy large packages of items you use a lot. It's cheaper to buy in bulk, in the long run.

☐ Eat at home to stay healthier and save money.

☐ Share meals with friends - maybe they will share with you!

☐ Buy second-hand clothes, or well-made clothes that won't go out of fashion too quickly. A cheap item of clothing isn't so cheap if you only get to wear it twice before it falls apart or goes out of fashion, whereas $90 may sound like a lot for a pair of jeans, but if you wear them 200 times, they're quite a bargain.

☐ Organize a clothing exchange with a group of like-minded friends: you all bring your unwanted clothes to someone's house, and everyone takes home whatever they think they can use. "New" clothes for free! Anything that's still unwanted can go to a charity store, or a used-clothing depot.

☐ Re-use things wherever possible: empty bread-bags can be tomorrow's sandwich bags; used and grubby grocery bags can become garbage bags; empty margarine or yogurt containers are great for storing leftover food in the fridge or freezer; empty shoeboxes can be used for wrapping presents or storing odds-and-ends; open large mailing envelopes carefully, and save them for when you need to mail something.

☐ Make gifts rather than buying them. If you *have* to buy some, decide on a spending limit ahead of time, and stick to it.

☐ Decide what you need and what you want. It's OK to buy some "wants" now and again, but make sure you know they are treats.

☐ If you are thinking of buying something, make a note of it and think about it for a couple of weeks or even months. After this period, reconsider. How many times did you think about it? Do you still really want it? Did you see any in the stores? How did the prices compare? Are any of the stores advertising sales?

☐ Paying with cash, rather than with a credit card, can save you money at some stores. Check this out, and factor it into the arithmetic when you are making a large purchase.

☐ Always check out the Sale racks first: you may find exactly what you want right there. And if you don't, you've at least given yourself a guideline against which to compare the costs of other items.

☐ Never let your credit card balance run over the "grace period" so you end up paying interest. And try to avoid getting cash advances on your credit card - you pay interest on those from the moment you draw the money.

☐ Walk or use public transport wherever possible. Delay buying a car until you are above the age of high insurance premiums. Even if you have a car, car-pool whenever possible to save on fuel and maintenance costs.

What are You Waiting For?

According to news reports, large numbers of twenty- and thirty-year-olds are migrating back to their parents' houses where they get a free roof over their heads and free use of the TVs, VCRs, gym equipment, and so forth. This trend is supposed to indicate that America has produced a new generation of freeloaders, who lack the gumption to go out into the world and make it on their own. There's a good side to this that we haven't heard much about, except in a recent headline in *The Wall Street Journal:* "Generation X Starts Saving for Retirement."

The gist of the story is that the freeloading twenty-somethings who belong to the so-called lost generation, or Generation X, have been quietly stashing away their loot. Apparently, there are more savers in this group than among their parents, the baby boomers who prefer buying things now to saving money for later. The Xers have realized that they can't count on social security to bail them out. They've watched their parents struggle to pay off credit-card debts, and they want to avoid repeating this mistake. They seek financial independence, and they're working toward it while they're still at home, with their parents picking up the tab.

This is a very positive development, and we can only hope that more teenagers will follow in the footsteps of the twenty-somethings and not fall into the familiar trap of buying an expensive car. Many kids can't wait to do this. As soon as they land that first steady job, they become slaves to the car payments. It's cool to drive around in a flashy new Camaro instead of a used Ford Escort, but that kind of cool is very costly in the long run. What's the price of cool? Consider the following two cases: Joe and Sally.

Joe gets a job as a clerk at Wal-Mart. He's living at home and saving every last dollar so he can make the $2,000 down payment on a $20,000 Camaro with the racing scoop on the hood. He takes out a car loan for the remaining $18,000. His parents have to sign for the loan, but Joe is making the payments. It's a five-year loan at 11.67 percent interest, so he sends $400 to the finance company every month. He cringes the first time he seals the envelope, kissing $400 goodbye, but he forgets all about that when he's driving around in the Camaro and his friends are telling him what a cool car it is.

A few months later, there are scratches on the door and stains on the carpet and nobody is oohing and aahing when the Camaro pulls into the parking lot. It's just another car by now, but Joe is stuck with the payments. To be able to afford the car and a date to ride in the car he works an extra night shift, which means he's too busy to get many dates.

At the end of five years, he's sick of the Camaro, which lost its cool a long time ago. He's finally paid off the car loan, which cost him an extra $6,000 in interest charges, so between the loan and the original purchase price, Joe has invested $26,000 in this car, not including taxes and fees, insurance premiums, gas, oil, and maintenance.

At this point, the Camaro has dents and stains and the engine sounds a bit rough. If he sold the thing he could get maybe $5,000 for it. So what he's got to show for his $26,000 investment is a $5,000 car that he doesn't even like anymore.

Sally also lives at home and works the Wal-Mart checkout line a few feet away from Joe, but she didn't buy a cool car. She took the $2,000 she'd saved up and bought a used Ford Escort. Since Sally paid cash, she didn't have car payments. So instead of sending $400 a month to the finance company, she invested $400 a month in a mutual fund for stocks.

Five years later, when Joe was mailing out his last car payment, the value of Sally's mutual fund had doubled. Between the doubling of the fund itself and the steady stream of $400 contributions to the fund, Sally has an asset of nearly $30,000. She also has the Escort, which gets her back and forth OK, and she never worries about the dents and stains because she never thought of her car as an investment. It's only transportation.

As we leave this economic morality tale, Sally has enough money to make a down payment on her own house and move out of her parents' house, while Joe continues to mooch. He's asked her out on a date, but she's taken a fancy to the real-estate agent who's showing her around.

Reading Mutual Funds

Recent prices of Investment funds supplied by Fundata Canada Inc. at 5:45 p.m. Nov. 27. Prices reported by funds are the net asset value per share or unit last calculated and are for information purposes only. Confirmation of price should be obtained from the fund. Chg - penny change from last valuation; D - distributed by fund sponsor; G - redemption charge; I - distributed by independent dealers; L - sales charge; N - no sales charge; O - optional front-end or redemption charge; R - eligible for RRSPs; Z - not available for sale; m - minimum purchase of $150,000; u - U.S. currency; x - ex-dividend; (n) - not a member of IFIC; (Date following fund denotes last valuation).

Fund	Load	RSP	Dist	Val	Chg
ABC FUNDS					
mAmer-Value 10/31	N		D	5.26	—
mFully-Mgd 10/31	N	R	D	8.84	—
mFund-Value 10/31	N	R	D	12.38	—
ACADIA INVESTMENT FUNDS					
Balanced 11/26	N	R		11.56	-.18
Bond 11/26	N	R		11.19	+.02
Mortgage 11/26	N	R		10.00	unch
ADMAX INTL. MANAGEMENTS					
Amer Sel Gth	O	Z		5.95	+.02
Asset All	O	R	I	14.28	+.01
Cdn Perf	O	R	I	7.84	+.02
Cdn Sel Gth	O	R	Z	5.84	+.01
Dragon 888	O		I	7.96	+.07
Europa	O		I	11.67	-.01
Glo Hlth	O		I	10.50	+.03
Intl	O		I	6.29	+.00
Korea	O		I	8.47	+.04
Nippon	O		I	12.06	+.01
Tiger	O		I	11.50	+.08
World Inc.	O	R	I	13.70	+.01
ADMAX INTL. MANAGEMENT U$					
uAmer Sel U$			Z	4.42	+.00

Fund	Load	RSP	Dist	Val	Chg
Small Cap	L	R	I	8.85	-.01
BISSETT					
Amer Equity	N		D	27.16	+.12
Bond	N	R	D	13.14	+.01
Cdn Equity	N	R	D	31.89	+.13
Dividend	N		D	16.79	+.09
Multinational	N		D	15.71	+.08
Retirement	N	R	D	16.04	+.04
Small Cap	N	R	D	32.54	+.09
BNP (CANADA) FUNDS					
Bond 11/26	N	R	D	11.36	+.02
Equity 11/22	N	R	D	37.00	—
BONHAM & CO INC. (n)					
SV Amer Equity	O			5.00	—
SV Cdn Equity	O	R		5.00	—
SV Glo Bal RRSP	O			5.00	—
SV Glo Equity	O			5.00	—
BPI MUTUAL FUNDS					
Amer Equ Valu	O		I	8.05	+.01
Amer Small Co	O		I	27.48	+.14
Asia Pacific	O		I	10.87	+.06
Cdn Balanced	O	R	I	5.35	unch
Cdn Bond	O	R	I	5.11	unch
Cdn Equ Value	O	R	I	9.02	unch
Cdn Resource	O	R	I	24.77	-.20
Cdn. Small Co	O	R	I	13.71	-.01
Emer Markets	O		I	11.56	+.06
Glo Bal RSP	O	R	I	15.79	+.01
Glo Equity	O		I	20.02	+.05
Glo RSP Bond	O	R	I	11.90	+.01
Glo Small Co	O		I	18.58	+.15
Income	O	R	I	11.48	+.03
BPI MUTUAL FUNDS U$					
uAmer Equ Val U$	O		I	5.98	-.01
uAmer Sml Co U$	O		I	20.41	+.05
uAsia Pacific U$	O		I	8.07	+.02
uEmer Markets U$	O		I	8.58	+.01
uGlo Equity U$	O		I	14.87	+.01
uGLo Small Co U$	O		I	13.80	+.07
BURGEONV					
Dolphin					

Fund	Load
Growth	
Income	
N.A. Equity	
Pacific Rim	
Special Equity	
FICADRE FUNDS	
Balanced 11/22	
Bond 11/22	
Equity 11/22	
Mortgage 11/22	
FIDELITY INVESTMENT	
Asset Manager	O
Cap Builder	O
Cdn Asset All	O
Cdn Bond	O
Cdn Gth Co	O
Cdn Income	O
Em Mkts Bond	
Em Mkts Pti	
Euro Growth	
Far East	
Growth Amer	
Intl Portfolio	
Japan Growth	
Latin American	
N.A. Income	
RSP Glo Bond	
Sm Cap Amer	
True North	
FIDELITY INVESTM	
uAsset Mgr U$	
uEm Mkts Bd U$	
uEm Mkts Pti U$	
uEuro Gth U$	
uFar East U$	
uGth Amer U$	
uIntl Pti U$	
uJapan Pti U$	
uLatin Amer U$ U$	

LEAVING HOME

Saying good-bye to Mom and Dad has its pitfalls

by Bill Sass

Tabitha Munro and Franki Harrogate were out on their own and ready to take on the world—until they got taken to the cleaners by the Hit-and-Run Roomie.

"She totally screwed us over," says Tabitha. She stole everything from shampoo to bank cards before she disappeared into the sunset.

"I'm still getting calls from the bank," says Franki. This roommate was older than Tabitha and Franki (18 and 17) and wasn't personally known to them.

"She was the close friend of a friend."

They couldn't absorb the loss and had to move back home—and are now getting ready for another stab at independent living, but this time they'll be asking a lot of questions before allowing anyone to move in with them.

The two women were part of a group of 12 students at Queen Elizabeth High School, some who have never moved out, some now living on their own and others who have either lived on their own and moved back home or, like Tabitha and Franki, plan on moving out again in the near future.

Mark Axhorn, an amiable football player resembling a brick wall with a smile, is in that latter category as well. He was planning another stab at independence a week after this interview after a first try didn't work out.

Tabitha Munro and Franki Harrogate learned the hard way the importance of questioning prospective roommates

"Freedom" wasn't quite what he expected. It translated more into worry—about money, roommates and food.

"It would keep me up nights," he said.

Money is the big worry. Most of the independents have to deal with the vagaries of part time work, no guaranteed hours and variable paycheques.

"You need a substantial amount of money." says Janet Wong, 18, who is

Claude and Paulette Hall plan to get their own place as soon as they can

In a unique situation which saw her parents move out "for business reasons," leaving her and her brother and assorted roommates with the family house. The parents pay the mortgage, utilities and food costs. She has to raise the money for tai kwan do lessons, orthopedic shoes, entertainment, transportation and any other extras.

"The first couple of months it was party time." Then things got tired—and a bit more serious. "It's hard to keep things in order."

Getting along and dealing with independence are things everyone has to learn, she said. "You have to find roommates who are dependable."

Friends are like strangers. Sometimes they make good roommates, sometimes not.

The learning process involves some strange problems and innovative solutions for these young people.

Claude, 19, and Paulette Hall, 17, are married—a rarity in any high school. They live with her parents now, but are planning to get their own place as soon as they can.

Claude has lived on his own and came across a lesson that most people don't think about until they are parents with older children. "If you've got a car, make sure you get transportation straightened out with your roommates." He found himself being

> *"The first couple of months it was party time."*
> *Then things got tired—and a bit more serious.*

awakened at 3 a.m. by roommates looking for a ride home.

Fouheir Berro, 19, lives with his brother and doesn't have to deal with a landlord—they bought a house instead.

"It's tough. I wouldn't advise it."

His big lesson: "It's the only time you figure out the value of money."

Beverly Walters is a life skills coach in the city and sees all the problems renters and roommates, new and old, can have.

"Somebody is always angry. It's the dynamics—even best friends don't make the best roommates."

Things like privacy (sometimes non-existent), food fights, income and rent and bill payment priorities wear and tear on apartment relationships, she said.

"You can't put as much faith in people as you can at home."

Walters' daughter Keirra, 26, has been on her own since she was 18, going from dormitory to apartment to her own house where she often takes in roomies/borders fresh from their parental homes.

"I've had some good and some really bad roommate situations."

A main key is flexibility, especially about the "small stuff" like who drinks the most milk or uses the most shampoo.

If it happens only occasionally, it's a small problem. If it happens regularly, the molehill grows into a mountain and the fights begin. "But you can't just holler at them like they're your brother or sister."

Another vital area of agreement is cleanliness. "You have to agree on a level of housekeeping—whether the house is spotless or not."

A lot of people just aren't ready for the world when it comes knocking at their door, she said.

"A lot of them can't deal with sales people, for instance. They can't say no to magazine or vacuum salesman—they've never had to deal with them and no one taught them."

Budgeting, grocery shopping and "separating the needs from the wants" are things people have to learn as they go along, if someone hasn't taught them at home, she said,...

"It can be pretty taxing."

Renting Without Confusion

After looking at two or more rental places, it's easy to be confused about what you have seen. It's always a good idea to take someone with you when you check out a place. If you are sharing with a room mate, go together. It's also a good idea to take along a checklist something like this. Then you can compare each place you have seen and make the best choice.

Address: _____

<u>COSTS:</u>

Rent $$ _____

Required Deposits - Security _____

         - Damage _____

Utilities - included in rent _____

     - not included in rent _____

Any other costs e.g. parking _____

Lease (sometimes called rental agreement or tenancy agreement)

Required/not required _____

Length _____

Can you sublet?
(Rent part of this place to another person) _____

Rent increases - how often? _____

         - how much? _____

Who is responsible for sidewalk clearing/yard upkeep? ____

Improvements - who does them? _____

         - who pays? _____

Restrictions - e.g. pets, guests? _____

Parking - for self? _____

     - for visitors? _____

Rate each of the following (1 to 5 - 1 is very poor, 5 is excellent

<u>THE PLACE</u>

❏ large enough

❏ bathroom is in good condition, clean, and all fixtures work

❏ kitchen is in good condition, clean, and all fixtures (stove, fridge, etc.) work

❏ no water stains under any sinks

❏ problems with pipes freezing?

❏ all lights and switches work

❏ no evidence of bugs, rodents

❏ entry door secure

❏ who has key access?

❏ balcony door secure with a good lock

hot water

❏ where is the source?

❏ is there enough?

laundry

❏ convenient and safe location

❏ condition of appliances

❏ cost

❏ rules for use

heating

- ❏ method of heating
- ❏ average cost
- ❏ are the controls in the apartment?
- ❏ if hot water-heated, is there any problem with pipes breaking?

air-conditioning

- ❏ is there air-conditioning?
- ❏ average cost
- ❏ are the controls in the apartment?

windows

- ❏ in good condition
- ❏ screens in place and in good condition
- ❏ open and close easily
- ❏ is there cross-ventilation?
- ❏ are curtains provided?
- ❏ if not, can curtain rods etc. be installed?
- ❏ is the view acceptable?

storage

- ❏ adequate storage in the apartment
- ❏ other available secured storage in building
- ❏ secured bike storage

THE BUILDING

noise

- ❏ in hallways
- ❏ elevator
- ❏ other tenants
- ❏ street noise

building condition

- ❏ lobby
- ❏ hallways
- ❏ stairs
- ❏ elevator, working and well-lit
- ❏ exterior and surrounding lot

safety

- ❏ buzzer access at main entrance
- ❏ all building entrances secured and well-lit
- ❏ well-lit parking area
- ❏ streets well-lit
- ❏ clearly marked and accessible fire escape routes
- ❏ CSA approved smoke detectors, alarms, fire extinguishers in hallways
- ❏ crime rate in neighbourhood
- ❏ if unit in basement or on first floor, do windows have secured metal grills?

CONVENIENCE FOR YOURSELF

- ❏ close to public transportation
- ❏ near work and/or school, grocery stores, other services you need

Other Comments:

_____

_____

_____

_____

_____

 **Tenant Insurance**

♦ Even if you think you have nothing to insure, once you are out on your own and renting a place, you should have personal property insurance to cover your personal contents and liabilities.

♦ Your contents, even if they don't seem to be much at first, can add up if you lose all of them to fire. Just think about losing all of your clothes, shoes, coats, household stuff, and furniture. Even if you have very little, the cost of replacing all of your stuff would probably add up to more than the cost of a Tenant's Insurance policy.

♦ You can be liable for any damages you cause. For example, if a fire starts in your apartment, you might be held responsible by the owner of the building and all the other tenants who have suffered losses. Forgetting to turn off the stove or having a friend drop a lit cigarette into a chair are all possibilities.

Beaten by the Clock

by Dave Finlayson

tick tick tick tick

The faster I go the behinder I get. It's an old line, usually followed by a few chuckles from those who can relate to rushing around being late for everything once in a while.

But it's no laughing matter for people who are always late, spending their whole lives looking at their watches in despair.

It's often a symptom of a problem with deeper emotional roots than just being disorganized, says Edmonton psychologist Paul Sussman.

And often they blame other people for their miserable, stressful lives.

"Usually the hand that launches the catapult full of claptrap into your life is your own. And coming to grips with your own personal issues is a big help," Sussman says.

And getting help, whether it's feedback from friends or sessions with a professional, can change your life in such a positive way, experts agree.

"People trust you more, are more likely to give you responsibility.

There's a more positive atmosphere all round," says Lorraine Breault, a city psychologist.

We all sometimes feel there aren't enough hours in a day.

In fact 62 per cent of workers in a U.S. survey said they feel pressed to accomplish everything they have to do, and only five per cent said they rarely or never feel rushed.

And everybody is different and can't easily be pigeon-holed, says Anne McGee-Cooper, co-author of *Time Management for Unmanageable People.*

For example, if you're a divergent, or right-brained, person who thinks about time in a flexible rather than rigid fashion, the classic rules of organizing your time won't work for you, she writes. And you can be highly successful, even if you have a messy desk, put everything in a pile instead of filing them, or rarely finish one task before moving onto another.

On a darker side though, there are those who mismanage time as a way to avoid an unpleasant task, shirk personal responsibility, resist change, sidestep new feelings, and avoid feeling close to others, says Dru Scott in her book *How to Put More Time in Your Life.*

There's also the satisfaction of defying authority.

"Some of us mismanage time to get attention or gain a sense of power," Scott says.

But we're not all candidates for psychoanalysis.

Breault says often a gentle pointing out by friends of how a person's lateness affects other people is all that's needed.

"Usually, lateness on its own is not that difficult to correct. But if there's an unresolved issue that's causing the behavior then it's more complex. The behavior won't change unless that issue is dealt with."

For many, following a few simple guidelines on time management can improve their lot considerably, whether they're working in an office or a mother at home with children.

One of the most important is that we shouldn't feel everything we do is a chore.

There should be something in our daily schedule we enjoy.

"I manage my time quite well but it always seems to be frenetic. But I try never to do things I don't like and that's a key for me," Sussman says.

You should also not feel you have to fill your calendar every day.

Set aside a certain amount of "spontaneous" time when you have nothing planned. It can be used to catch up, regroup, or just relax.

Sussman likes to meditate and so that regularly goes into his day book.

"It's OK to do relaxing, self-serving activities and if you feel sheepish or ashamed about it you should seek some help," Sussman says.

He believes shame is at the heart of neurotic behavior such as chronic lateness, not guilt as Sigmund Freud, the father of psychoanalysis, suggested.

"Guilt comes from doing something wrong; shame comes from being something wrong, and wanting to hide. And it usually comes from something in their childhood making them feel that way."

It can come from being made to feel inadequate, or even being physically or sexually abused.

But whatever they try to do in life they run smack into their shame, and there are predictable patterns to how they deal with it.

They make jokes (I'd like to procrastinate but I can't seem to find the time), or they numb out their feelings, pretending there are no issues.

But everybody has issues; getting them to admit it is another matter.

Sussman says he started off a recent seminar for businesspeople on time management by telling them the session was about logical, good and healthy ways to manage their time more effectively; and if any of them were in a time crunch because they couldn't say no, or tried to do too many things in too many different areas, then they should seek professional help.

"Many looked disappointed. They wanted someone to tell them what to do about all the things they cram into their 24-hour day. Nobody can do that…

And in case you're one of those superior people who despise chronic latecomers, you're not off the hook either.

Showing such an obsessive amount of intolerance could mean you have a problem, especially if you punish the offenders disproportionately to their crime.

"These people believe they're asserting their power, when it's actually dysfunctional," Breault says.

Have a nice day.

Tips for Better Time Management

- Use the "Swiss Cheese" approach. Poking holes in daunting jobs reduces them to manageable size.
- Set priorities. Don't just work down your list in order, but put A (must do), B (should do) or C (could do) against each item.
- Practise saying no. Start small, promising yourself to say no once a week and building up until it becomes habitual.
- Make "down time" as important as "on time." Women in particular have trouble setting aside moments for themselves. Try practising the sentence "this is my time" until it comes easily.
- Learn the art of letting go. When a list becomes too overwhelming it's time to take a good look at what you can realistically expect to accomplish. Drop a couple of low-priority items completely, and delegate others.

Signs There May Be a Problem

If you're always a couple of minutes late for meetings, that's probably a time-management problem that can be fixed.

But if any of the following sound familiar, there may be an underlying emotional issue that needs addressing. It doesn't necessarily mean you've got a serious problem, but you should consider getting help.

- You have difficulty arranging your priorities on a daily basis — despite having a list — and end up doing little or nothing.
- You have difficulty saying no because you want everybody to like you. So anybody who wants some of your time gets it.
- You stack so many things into your schedule you'd need a 48-hour day to accomplish everything, and you feel guilty if you try to cut down the list.
- You're late because you're angry with the people who make demands on your time. Instead of confronting them, you take the passive-aggressive approach by making them wait.
- You find it impossible to take time for yourself during a busy day.
- You are late, even for things you enjoy, because you find having to be somewhere at a certain time stressful.
- You're always late because it gives you a feeling of control.

FAQ Procrastination: the art of putting things off

Most of what you put off will still have to be done in the future - avoiding and procrastinating probably waste more time than getting the task done. To deal with your own procrastination, try

1. Start - once you are into a task, you may find it easier to keep going.

2. Deal with things when they happen. If you write a cheque, record it while you are standing there, if you use a credit card, don't toss the receipt: put it in your wallet and have a place at home for storing them all together until the bill arrives.

3. Expect delays - nothing gets done in the time you allow for it. (Ever had that happen to you with a term paper?) So start earlier than you think you need to.

The Big Bucks Business Behind

Rock Concerts

Yearning for U2?
Nuts about Nelly?
Crazy for Creed?

When the bands come to town, the fans want to be there. But big concerts don't just happen. They're packaged, promoted, and sold, like other products. Here's how . . .

Selling the Concerts

If you saw Dylan on Beverly Hills 90210 sporting a Rolling Stones cap, you've been caught in concert hype. To help sell its 1994 Voodoo Lounge tour to a younger generation of rockers, the fifty-something Stones hooked up with the twenty-something Beverly Hills 90210 crowd for a prime-time episode. The plot centered around whether or not members of the 90210 gang would attend the band's concert. Swayed by Dylan's praise of the Stones as "the masters of rock," they eventually decide to go. That leads to exclusive 90210 footage of the Stones in concert. ("At least it wasn't the Beverly Hillbillies," said guitarist, Keith Richards.)

Not every band can tout its tour on prime-time TV. But many can get radio stations to promote their concerts by giving them free tickets. The stations, in turn, give those tickets to listeners through call-in contests. But first…disc jockeys hype the concert and ticket-giveaway over and over before finally inviting fans to phone in for the freebies. That builds excitement for the concert and the station — and keeps listeners tuned in.

Music stores and record companies may invite fans to sign up for contests in stores. Fans flock to the stores with hopes of winning premium prizes like backstage passes, concert jackets, even autographed guitars. The music merchants, meanwhile, hope that all the excitement will spill over into their cash registers while fans are in the store.

What pumped-up fan could resist buying a band's album when it's strategically placed by a contest sign-up?

Of course, with any kind of giveaway contest, only a few lucky listeners can win the ballyhooed freebies. The thousands of other fans who've been revved up by the hype will have to buy their tickets!

And Now, for a Word From Our Sponsors

But the selling doesn't end when you buy your ticket. Products might be advertised on concert tickets, programs, even splashed across banners on stage. Companies often sponsor (pay money to) a performer, in return for advertising their products wherever the concert goes.

Those "masters of rock" the Stones proved to be "masters of industry" as well. The band started the sponsorship trend in 1981 by accepting one million dollars from Jovan perfume to help pay for its tours. Since then, many performers have followed suit: Melissa Etheridge has been sponsored by VH-1, Anita Baker by USAir, and Woodstock '94 by Pepsi and Häagen-Dazs. In its 1995 Superfest, Budweiser sponsored Boyz II Men, Mary J. Blige, TLC, Montell Jordan, and Soul for Real. And in 1994, the Stones, old pros at the sponsorship game, collected more than $24-million from Volkswagen, Budweiser, VH-1, Visa, and MasterCard for the Voodoo Lounge tour.

But some bands feel that associating their music with a product cheapens their image, and they refuse to have sponsors. In 1992, U2 turned down sponsors for its flashy Zoo TV tour. Live recently turned down a deal with Budweiser, which would have put beer ads on its tickets and on stage.

The Story Behind Ticket Prices

That $23.75 for a Cranberries concert might take a big chunk out of a budget. But that's peanuts compared to the $115 some folks forked over for the Eagles reunion tour. Ticket prices depend on everything from how much it costs to put on the concert to how much money the performers want to make.

Big shows have big expenses. Madonna's Blonde Ambition tour, for instance, cost enough to turn anybody's hair white: one and a half million dollars a week (about $500,000 per concert). How can shows cost so much? Huge stages and sound systems have to be put up, taken down, and transported by truck or plane. The band and production crew run up hefty hotel and food bills, in addition to their salaries. There's also the cost of:

■ Insurance. How much depends on how rowdy (and risky) the concert

may be. Insurance for rap and heavy metal concerts usually costs more than for a country music concert.

■ Security. So the band won't have to use their insurance.

■ Rent. How much the concert site charges depends mainly on how big it is. A place that seats 12,000 might charge about $5,000, or a certain percent of ticket sales.

■ Performers. The stars collect a percentage of the profit from ticket sales, or a guaranteed amount of money, or both.

■ Promoter. The person who arranges the whole deal usually gets a percentage of the profits — if there are any! If tickets sell poorly, the promoter still has to pay the performers, and cover the rest of the expenses. (That makes promoting concerts a very risky business.)

Ticket prices can also depend on the promoters and performers themselves. If they think fans will spend a lot, chances are they'll ask for it. Fans of the Eagles, Barbra Streisand, or the Rolling Stones tend to be older and have more money than kids. They're often willing and able to pay from $50 to $350 for a ticket.

Tacking on a Service Charge

You've barely saved up enough for a concert ticket when, surprise! You have to pay another $2.50 to $8.00 "service charge" on top of the ticket price! Ticket-selling agencies, like TicketMaster, don't make money from the ticket itself. They tack on a service charge to cover the cost of maintaining their computers, renting office space, and paying phone bills and salaries — and, of course, to make some profit. You can sometimes avoid service charges by buying directly from the concert hall's box office.

Don't Forget the Souvenirs!

Be prepared to cough up more cash if you want a band's T-shirt, poster, or some other concert souvenir. Those T-shirts cost the souvenir-sellers around $4, but you'll have to pay from $15 to $35 for one. Where does all that money go?

The concert hall or stadium gets about 35 cents of every dollar spent on souvenirs. The band gets a cut of the rest, with some groups collecting up to 40 cents of every dollar. When Guns N' Roses opened for Aerosmith, it took in a quarter of a million dollars a night on merchandise — much more than it was paid to play.

The souvenir-seller also takes a cut, enough to cover operating costs and earn a profit. No wonder a $4 shirt can end up costing $35!

The good news: Some bands are demanding lower souvenir prices. Pearl Jam put a $20 limit on its T-shirts. Offspring fans can get $12 shirts, thanks to the band's insistence that the concert hall take a smaller cut.

Concert Smarts

■ **Getting good seats.** If the concert has general admission (unassigned seats), you'll have to camp out in line hours before the show starts to snag the best seats. If it's reserved seating, hitting the ticket line early can help, but may not guarantee you great seats. That's because the same tickets are available at every ticketing outlet in town through computer link-ups. There may be 50 other lines at 50 other ticket outlets. Often those front-row seats have already been given to VIPs or radio stations anyway.

■ **Backstage passes.** Unless you know the band or its promoter, you probably have to work at the concert hall or win passes from a contest to get backstage. But backstage passes may not be as cool as you

AP Photo/Emile Wamsteker

them and their fans, so they limit the number of tickets each person can buy to keep scalpers from buying blocks of tickets to sell.

- **Plan your transportation.** If your driver isn't with you at the show, agree on a pick-up time and spot with your ride. Choose a well-lit spot, close to people.

- **Bring phone numbers and quarters or cellphone.** Have plenty of change and at least two phone numbers where you know you'll be able to reach someone.

- **Mosh alert!** Slamming around in the crowd in front of the stage may seem like fun, but it's dangerous. Three people died and thousands injured in moshing accidents. The worst injuries came from crowd surfing and stage diving. Save that for water!

Now Hear This

Concerts may be a blast, but they can also blast away your hearing. Just ask Pete Townsend of The Who, Jason Newstead, Sting and Elton John, Eric Clapton, and Ted Nugent, who all complain of hearing loss.

Tiny hair cells in the cochlea (the fluid-filled part of the inner ear) conduct sound to the brain. Very loud sound can damage and destroy those hair cells. Less than 30 minutes of a loud concert (120 decibels) can cause damage. Ringing in the ears after a concert is a sign of possible damage. Take the advice of punk rock musician Kathy Peck, who founded HEAR (Hearing Education and Awareness for Rockers) as a result of her own hearing loss: Pick up some ear plugs from a drug or hardware store before going to a concert. They'll soften the sound, not block it out completely. If you don't have ear plugs, try toilet tissue. (Just make sure the wad isn't too small.)

Sometimes you may be lucky enough to get something for free as part of a tour promotion. More often, though, you'll have to shell out some cash.

think. "Bands usually stay in seclusion in their dressing room," said Mike Oliviero, promotions manager of radio station 98 Rock in Tampa Bay, Florida. If you do get to meet the band, "it's usually a quick handshake. Some bands won't even sign autographs or let you take photos."

- **Sold out?** If the ticket outlet says the concert is sold out, try the main box office. Sometimes it will open up extra sections to a sold-out show. But avoid scalpers (people who resell tickets for much higher prices at the concert site.) Bands like REM believe scalpers steal from

TEEN GAMBLING

Can You Bet on It?

Super Stock

E ver bought a lottery ticket? Bet on a one-on-one basketball game or a school team? Ever scratched a ticket, placed a computer wager on a national sports event, filled in a raffle ticket, gone to bingo, or played a card game for pennies with your family? Many people think these pastimes are harmless although they are all forms of gambling. However, for some people, including some teens, gambling becomes a real problem - an addiction. In fact, problem gambling for teens is growing in Canada; it is increasing at three times the adult rate.

What part does gambling play in your life? Some people believe that gambling in any form is morally wrong and don't do it. Others believe that some forms are harmless and fun social activities. And still others love to gamble - no matter the form. It is up to you to make a choice about whether or not you gamble or what forms of gambling you play. To make that personal choice,

- decide how you feel about gambling before you are in a situation where there is a opportunity to gamble;

- remember that you can choose not to gamble in any form and at any time, and you can certainly choose not to gamble to be part of the group;

- know that you do not need to gamble to have a good time;

- if you choose to gamble, set yourself a limit. Know how much you are willing to lose and walk away from the game if that amount is gone. If you are gambling with others, agree on the limits of the game beforehand and stick to them. Know when to stop;

- don't ever borrow money to gamble;
- don't gamble illegally; know the age restrictions;
- don't combine gambling with drinking or drugs; they impair your judgement and your self-control;
- don't gamble to impress other people, relieve stress, or to score that next big win.

How can you recognize a gambler in trouble?

Does the person
- talk about gambling and boast about the winnings; being excited about gambling but not discussing losses?
- borrow money frequently?
- complain about more debts than usual; debts seem to be growing?
- spend more time, including noon hours, at the phone or at the lottery counter?
- have new, unexplained absences from school or work?
- seem to run out of money quickly?
- seem to feel guilty about gambling or tend to deny it?
- chase the next "big win" by gambling more frequently or placing bigger bets; pinning hope on the next big win?
- have mood swings - "up" when winning and "down" when losing?
- lie or refuse to talk about gambling?
- usually prefer gambling to other social activities?
- gamble for the challenge and the excitement of winning?

The truth is that, over time, a gambler will lose more than win. If someone you care about is a problem gambler, there are a couple of things you can do. Tell your friend that you are concerned about their gambling, but that you will no longer cover for them at school or work, for absences or lack of work done. Make it clear that you will not be lending the person any more money. Tell the gambler that you are concerned and that there are help groups for gamblers such as Gamblers' Anonymous as well as other local community groups.

 **Problem Gamblers...**

- gamble until the last dollar is gone;
- believe that after losing, they can go back and win back the losses;
- believe that after winning, it is important to go back as soon as possible to win more;
- gamble to pay off debts or pay bills;
- take time away from other things with family or friends to gamble;
- borrow money from other people;
- sell things to get money to gamble;
- feel guilty about gambling;
- believe that it is possible to win by knowing the game well and being smart;
- believe that persistence is necessary; "If I haven't won in a while, I am due for a win soon";
- end up stealing from their family or shoplifting.

Nothing Stays the Same Forever

Change, as you know, is inevitable. Some changes we can plan for. If we know that something is going to happen we usually have some idea how it's going to affect us. Maybe your roommate's planning to get married and move out. You have warning. You can plan. You can decide whether you can afford to stay on in the apartment, whether you'll have to look for a new roommate, or whether you'd rather move somewhere else.

But sometimes changes happen suddenly. You don't get a lot of warning when you're hit by a bus and your broken leg means you can't wait tables at the local steakhouse. No more wages or tips. How are you going to pay the bills, eat, and live in the style to which you have become accustomed? Sitting home and sulking isn't going to solve your problem.

So, how can you handle the changes you don't know are going to happen? Here are a few tips:

1) One really good way is to have a bit of money saved away for emergencies - enough to keep you alive for a couple of months.

2) See if your family and friends can help you, perhaps by filling in your shifts at work until you can get up and about again.

3) Maybe explaining the emergency to the people concerned (e.g., your boss, the landlord or the bank) may allow them to be a bit more flexible, provided that they know you will pay as soon as you can.

4) You may want to change your lifestyle and spend less money for a while. This isn't the time to buy a new car or stereo!

The moral of this story is, prepare for what you can, and be flexible to handle what you can't.

Take Some Credit
maintaining good credit rating
by Joanne Thomas Yaccato

On your journey to financial independence, the first stop is debt control. How do you rate as a borrower?

The care and feeding of your credit rating is a vital part of financial literacy and independence. The trouble is, most Canadians don't have a clue what their current credit rating is—until they blow it. Only when they're refused credit, or collide with bill collectors, or have to reestablish themselves after divorce or widowhood, do most folks realize they're in trouble.

The usual culprit is credit-card abuse. I know whereof I speak. In my 20s, I single-handedly and unknowingly destroyed my credit rating. (Thank the follies of youth, a broken ankle that cost me a job, and complete ignorance of the principles of credit.) As a result, I became an instant expert on credit at 28, after having my credit

card refused—and confiscated—at a business lunch. Here's what I learned:

Your credit record begins the minute your first credit application has been approved. That's an application in your own name, based on your own financial circumstances. Though it's less common today, there are still many women who depend on their husband's credit as opposed to having their own. If you're one of them, you may not exist with the credit bureau. This can be dangerous later, should you find yourself dealing with divorce or the death of your husband.

The way to establish a good credit rating is to borrow money—even as little as $500—and pay it back on time. The way to keep a good rating is to make all payments, even it it's the minimum, on time and not take on more debt than you can handle. Every 30

days, each of your creditors passes along information to the credit bureau about your outstanding balance, missed payments and current credit rating with that company. The bureau, in turn, passes along this information to anyone to whom you apply for credit.

So it's not the credit bureau that establishes your rating. Rather, each company you've dealt with gives you an "R" rating, beginning with R0 (as soon as you've been approved for credit) and ranging from R1 to R9, depending on your performance as a debtor.

An R1 rating is like an A+ in school—it should be treasured. R1 means you make your payments within 30 days. R2 means you pay in 30-60 days, and are a payment behind. And so on down to R5 (you're 120 days overdue, or more). You don't want to know higher R numbers, which mean the company has taken steps to get their

Scot Ritchie/Three in a Box

...having my credit-card refused and confiscated at a business lunch

money. Especially not R9, which means the collection agency is after you.

It's amazing how easy it is to get downgraded: even if you go one day over the 30-day time frame you're considered a payment behind and lose your coveted R1 score, and so on down the scale. You do not get informed when this happens. Its around R3 that your potential credit grantor starts wondering if you're a little light in the financial discipline department.

And don't think that paying off delinquent amounts get you in the clear again. Your low rating remains unchanged, and the record of missed or late payments becomes part of your credit file for seven years, after which it is removed by law.

Each company has different criteria for approving new applications. You need a flawless credit rating to get a platinum American Express card; the same is not necessary to get cheque cashing privileges at the supermarket. Other factors include your income and where you live: a neurosurgeon in Winnipeg's exclusive Tuxedo neighborhood gets brownie points on the "consistent income" and "stable lifestyle" checklists.

Although credit bureaus are under provincial jurisdiction and are required to maintain accurate records, their information is only as good as what's given to them. You have the right to dispute what's on your record. Equifax Canada, the country's largest credit bureau, handles over 800,000 customer requests for file inspections annually. You can get this information by mail (call your credit bureau for details) or by visiting your local office. Be prepared to show two pieces of photo ID.

Five years after my embarrassing lunch, I applied for a bank loan and was turned down—because of that confiscated credit card. I visited Equifax, spoke to the issuing bank and (because of my newfound respectability as a financial adviser and because the debt had long been repaid) got my file amended.

I often wish that credit had been taught in high school—financial education deserves at least as much attention as the three Rs. Certainly, knowing the state of your credit file—before it becomes a problem—is as important as knowing what your RRSP is worth and how much your life is insured for.

If the following doesn't prompt you into action, nothing will. In 1991, CBC-TV's Market Place asked Canadians to go to their credit bureaus to find out their status. Of those who did, 47 percent found inaccuracies—and 13 percent found errors big enough to have credit declined. Are you one of them?

BARTERING

Think of the word "barter". Do you get an image of stone age people swapping a bearskin for a handful of flints? Or someone shovelling a driveway in return for a ride to school or work? Think again. These days, bartering is big business for many large companies.

Bartering doesn't have to be just between two people, or two companies. You can join an international organization and trade with other members using cards rather like credit cards. The organization keeps track of all the exchanges done among its members, and issues each member with a monthly statement. So you can use the goods or services from one company, and provide something to another company, with no money changing hands. You can find out about these organizations on the Internet.

BUT: Everything traded must be assigned a dollar value, and GST (plus PST, if applicable) must be paid to the government just as if it were a regular sale. Similarly, the value of bartered goods and services is considered as part of your income, so is subject to income tax.

Bartering may have originated in the stone ages, but it's come a long way since then!

The Basics of Banking $

W hile saving is a good idea, jars of coins under your desk or bills rolled up into a sock in a drawer can't really get you very far. You need to choose a financial institution, a place where you can put your money. There are several reasons for doing this:

- it's a safe place for your money—a place where you can't lose it or have it stolen
- it will help you save money because your cash is not always right at hand for spur-of-the-moment spending ideas
- you can make money, if the type of account you have pays interest
- if you have a chequing account, you can pay bills with cheques that can be mailed or cashed only by the person named on the cheque
- having one or more accounts will give you good references when you need a loan or want to get a credit card. This may be the most important reason for banking at some institution.

Financial Institutions

In Canada, there are several different types of financial institutions.

★ Chartered banks can be found across Canada. To be a chartered bank means that the institution has been issued a charter from the Federal Bank Act. Simply, a chartered bank has been licensed by the government of Canada. All the everyday activities done by a chartered bank we commonly refer to as banking. Each depositor is protected by the CDIC, the Canada Deposit Insurance Corporation to a total of $60,000.

★ Trust companies are companies that act as a trustee, being the intermediary between borrowers and lenders. Both federally- and provincially-registered trust companies exist in Canada.

★ Credit unions are provincial co-operative saving and lending associations that are owned by their members. These can be CDIC insured as well.

★ Even some investment companies offer some of these banking transactions as a service to their investors.

How it All Works

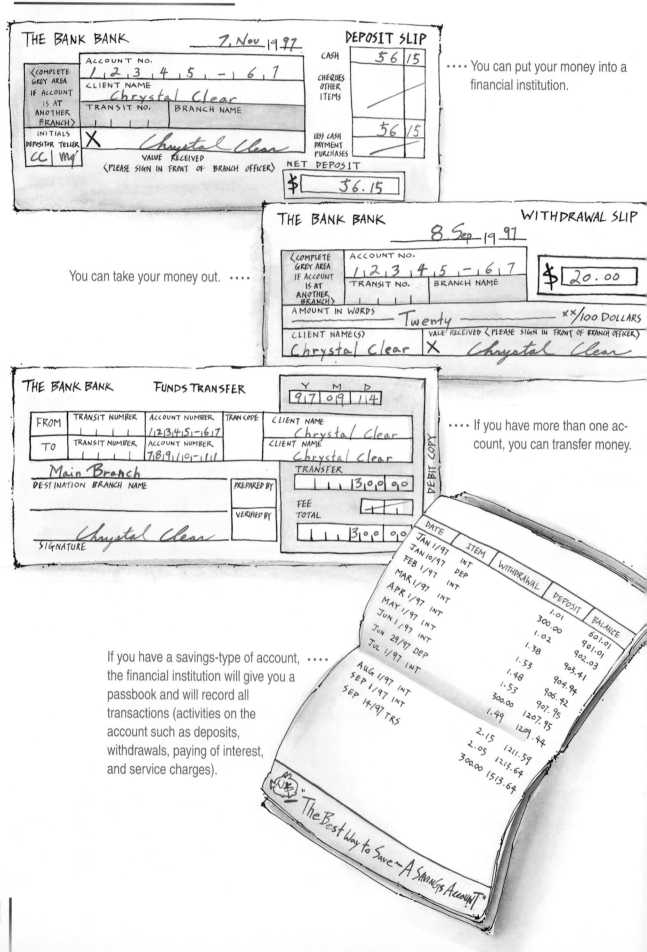

You can put your money into a financial institution.

You can take your money out.

If you have more than one account, you can transfer money.

If you have a savings-type of account, the financial institution will give you a passbook and will record all transactions (activities on the account such as deposits, withdrawals, paying of interest, and service charges).

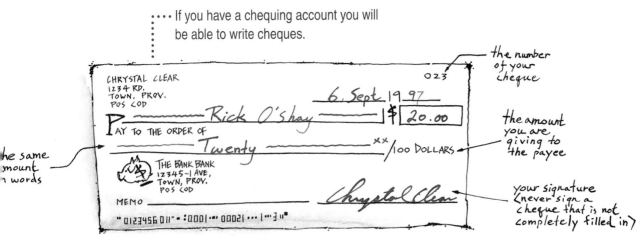

If you have a chequing account you will be able to write cheques.

- the number of your cheque
- the amount you are giving to the payee
- the same amount in words
- your signature (never sign a cheque that is not completely filled in)

CHRYSTAL CLEAR
1234 RD.
TOWN, PROV.
POS COD

6. Sept 19 97

PAY TO THE ORDER OF Rick O'shay $ 20.00

Twenty xx /100 DOLLARS

THE BANK BANK
12345-1 AVE,
TOWN, PROV.
POS COD

MEMO Chrystal Clear

023

⑆0123456 0⑈ ⑉0001⑉ 00021 ⑈ I⑈ 3 ⑈

Every time you write a cheque or deposit money into your chequing account, you need to record the transaction in your cheque register. It's almost impossible to recall three or four transactions over a few days so it is important to record each action when you do it. The transaction can also be recorded on the memo line of the cheque.

DATE	CHEQUE N°	CHEQUES ISSUED TO OR DESCRIPTION OF DEPOSIT	CHEQUE AMOUNT	✓	DEPOSIT AMOUNT	Deduct Cheque Add deposit	BALANCE FWD. 620 25
5 SEP		To Cash Deposit			56 15	CHEQUE – DEPOSIT+	
		FOR from paycheque				BALANCE ►	676 40
6 SEP	23	To RICK O'SHAY	20 00			CHEQUE – DEPOSIT+	
		FOR money he loaned me				BALANCE ►	656 40
8 SEP		To Cash Withdrawal	20 00			CHEQUE – DEPOSIT+	
		FOR for movie				BALANCE ►	636 40
12 SEP		To Cash deposit			56 15	CHEQUE – DEPOSIT+	
		FOR from paycheque				BALANCE ►	692 55
14 SEP		To TRANSFER	300 00			CHEQUE – DEPOSIT+	
		FOR to saving accounts				BALANCE ►	392 55
4 OCT		To Service fee	1 50			CHEQUE – DEPOSIT+	
		FOR				BALANCE ►	391 05

THE BANK BANK
12345 – 1 AVE,
TOWN, PROV,
POS COD

CHEQUING ACCOUNT

TRANSIT No.
Chrystal Clear
1234 Road,
TOWN PROV
POS COD

Account Statment

Account No.   Statement Period   Enclosed items Page
12345 –67   5 Sep 1997 to 4 Oct 1997   6   1

Date	Description	Withdrawals	Deposits	Balance
	Balance Forward			620.25
5 Sept	cash deposit		56.15	676.40
6 Sept	cheque #23	20.00		656.40
8 Sept	cash withdrawal	20.00		636.40
12 Sept	cash deposit		56.15	692.55
14 Sept	transfer	300.00		392.55
4 Oct	service free	1.50		391.05

Once a month, you receive a statement indicating the transactions you have made during the month. You need to reconcile the statement. That means you check your statement with the records you have written in your check register, the book that comes with your cheques.

Of course, different financial institutions have slightly different-looking forms, but there are some important general guidelines for use.

- Don't ever sign any form that is not completely filled out, especially cheques
- Use lines before and after the written amount on a cheque so that no numbers can be added by someone else.
- Never endorse (sign the back of your cheque) until you are just about to cash or deposit it. Endorsing a cheque allows anyone to cash it.

FAQ Banking

- Financial institutions can pay you interest because they lend your money to people for mortgages and loans which have an interest rate charged to the borrowers.

- Having one or more bank accounts is a good way of establishing a credit rating or indicating that you are responsible with money when you go to apply for a credit card.

- There are several different types of accounts. A straight savings account probably pays the highest interest rate on your money but charges you for withdrawals. It is the best account for saving money for a longer period of time. Choose a "no frills", "no chequing" account because they often have a higher interest rate. Also, some savings accounts increase the interest paid with a minimum balance held in the account.

- A chequing account allows you to put money in and withdraw it with very little or no charge. It is probably the best type of account for day-to-day use of your money - withdrawing cash and paying bills. Some chequing accounts charge a service fee and then allow unlimited number of withdrawals. Some chequing accounts charge for withdrawals after a set number of free withdrawals within the month. Some accounts are a combination of both savings and chequing accounts. You can ask questions about the accounts available - asking what interest rate is paid and what fees are charged - and choose the one that is best for you.

- Avoid NSF (Not Sufficient Funds) charges. This happens when you write a cheque for more money than is in your account. Not only will the cheque "bounce" (not be honoured), you will also be charged an extra fee for writing a NSF cheque. (That's one good reason for keeping your cheque register up-to-date.)

- There are other services, not financial institutions, which offer to cash cheques for you but they charge you for the service, usually a percentage which can range from 4% or higher of the cheque's total value. This means that you are paying someone else your money to cash your cheque. A banking institution can give you a much better deal. This goes for your pay cheques and other cheques written out to you.

- You may be able to use debit cards with your bank account. Debit cards are really just another way to remove money from your account. When you are paying for something, you "swipe" your card (run your card through a machine), and your money is transferred immediately from your account to the store. The advantage of a debit card is that it helps control your spending as it will not debit an account that does not have enough money in it.

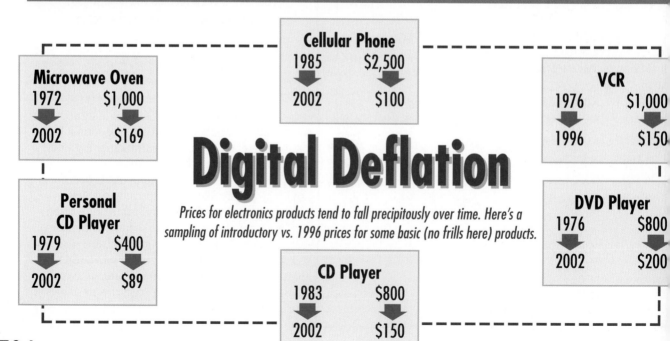

Microwave Oven
1972 — $1,000
→
2002 — $169

Cellular Phone
1985 — $2,500
→
2002 — $100

VCR
1976 — $1,000
→
1996 — $150

Personal CD Player
1979 — $400
→
2002 — $89

DVD Player
1976 — $800
→
2002 — $200

CD Player
1983 — $800
→
2002 — $150

Digital Deflation

Prices for electronics products tend to fall precipitously over time. Here's a sampling of introductory vs. 1996 prices for some basic (no frills here) products.

Electronic Banking

If you lose your card, tell the bank immediately. You may be held responsible for any transactions that happen on your account prior to the bank being informed.

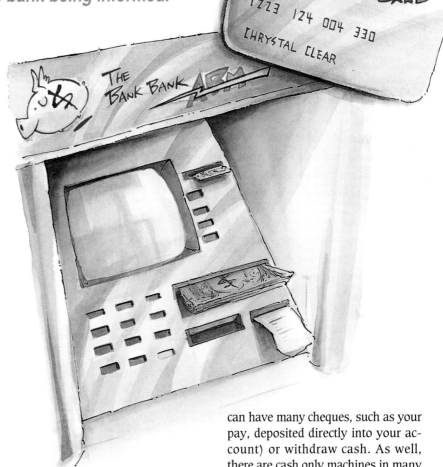

Automated Banking Machines

ABMs allow you to deposit and withdraw money, transfer money from one account to another, and pay bills. To use an ABM you need a plastic card coded with a number and your name. You also need a Personal Identification Number (PIN). This is not printed on the plastic card. It is a number, either given to you by the bank or chosen by you, that will be needed every time you use the machine. Your PIN number is your protection - it is the only way that anyone can get into your accounts even if they have your plastic card. So, it is very important that no one else knows your PIN number - so don't tell anyone, even best friends! One big advantage of ABMs is that most of them are open 24 hours a day, 7 days a week.

Using an ABM is really simple. Insert your card and follow the instructions. It will ask you for your PIN number and then ask you what you want to do. When the transaction is finished, the ABM will give you a receipt - that's what you use to update your cheque register - and your card. Don't forget to take both!

Telephone Banking

In Canada, about 85% of service delivery is done on telephone lines. This includes ABMs and now telephone banking which has become available to almost everyone with a touch tone phone. Anyone with a bank account can use telephone banking if it is of-

fered by their financial institution. There is a monthly fee for this service.

When you sign on to this service, you provide the bank with the account numbers of all the bills you wish to pay: utilities, credit cards, and many other fees that are regularly paid. Then you can use the telephone to do banking business, by punching numbers to pay these bills. You can also transfer money from one account to another. The only reason you would go to an ABM would be to deposit cheques (and don't forget that you

can have many cheques, such as your pay, deposited directly into your account) or withdraw cash. As well, there are cash only machines in many places which allow you to withdraw money. With some financial institutions, loans can even be applied for and granted by telephone.

Computer Banking

More and more, you are able to do your banking by computer. Usually this is not done over the Internet. Instead, usually there is a special inscription for security which is issued to you by the bank. This allows for protection of your important numbers.

FAQ Automated Banking and Direct Payment: Ten Tips on security

1. Your ABM/debit card is the key to your account(s). It is for your personal use **only.** Keep your card in a safe place and never "lend" it to anyone, including friends and family members.

2. Conducting an ABM or debit transaction requires **both** your access card and the corresponding Personal Identification Number (PIN). Protect your PIN, it is your electronic signature. Don't write it down — memorize it.

3. If you are selecting a PIN, always avoid the obvious e.g. your name, your telephone number, your date of birth, etc.

4. Never disclose your PIN to anyone. **No one** from a financial institution, the police or a merchant will ever ask you for your PIN. You are the **only** person who should know it.

5. Always conduct your ABM transactions when and where you feel most secure. If you are uncomfortable about using the machine for any reason, do it later or go to another location.

6. To ensure privacy when conducting an ABM or debit transaction, use your hand or body as a shield to prevent others from observing you entering your PIN.

7. After completing an ABM or debit transaction, remember to take your card and, if provided, your transaction record.

8. When making a withdrawal from an ABM, count the cash received and put it away immediately.

9. If your card is lost, stolen or is retained by an ABM, notify your financial institution **immediately.** Most institutions offer 1-800 telephone numbers and/or 24-hour service for lost or stolen cards.

10. Robbery rarely occurs at ABMs but if it should happen, remember that your safety comes first. Always report the incident to the police and to your financial institution.

HOW TO SAVE $500
without really trying

- Always pay yourself first by putting some amount in a savings account before you use the rest of the paycheque.

- If you have a part-time job or other regular source of income, put $10 a week (or $20, if you are paid every two weeks) into a savings account. Open a separate account for this if you already have a savings account at the bank. If your work cheque is direct-deposited (that's when you don't actually see the cheque but your employer gives it directly to the bank), ask the bank to transfer the amount directly into your special account. Then forget about it for a year. Don't forget about your other savings account though; still pay yourself savings into that account.

- Empty the coins from your change purse or wallet into a jar. (This drives the Bank of Canada crazy because it takes coins out of circulation! But, hey, they won't be out of circulation that long.) When the jar is full, roll the coins—you can buy paper or plastic rollers to do this—and then deposit the rolls of coins into that special savings account at the bank. Because they can really add up, you will have to decide whether loonies and two-nies go into that jar. Whatever you decide, no taking money from the jar.

- Anytime you buy something on sale, put the difference between the regular price and the sale price into the jar.

- Use your budget to identify the expenses you have that are not all that important to you. Bank the money you would have spent on these items.

Energy$aver Checklist

Rate yourself! This handy Energy$aver checklist can help you save money. Give yourself one point for each tip you follow and check your score below.

Appliances

- Check EnerGuide rating when buying appliances.
- Wash full loads of laundry.
- Avoid keeping the fridge door open.
- Locate fridge away from the stove and radiators.
- Clean the coils on the back of your fridge.
- Check fridge and freezer door seals.
- Empty and unplug fridge during vacations.
- Defrost fridge and freezer regularly.
- Set thermostats at 4°C (40°F) for fridges and -18°C (0°F) for freezers.
- Use oven to cook multiple items.
- Turn oven off 1/2 hour before finishing time.
- Match pots to stove element size.
- Cover pots and use lower heat settings.

Lighting

- Use fluorescent and task lighting where possible.
- Clean light bulbs and fixtures regularly.
- Use dimmer switches for some lights.
- Use lower wattage bulbs for general lighting.
- Use timers on lights during vacations.
- Turn off TV and lights when not in use.

Draftproofing

- Check caulking around windows.
- Ensure all windows have at least two panes.
- Check weatherstripping around your doors and windows.
- Install draft-enders on wall outlets.
- Check the attic hatch for tightness and airseal.

Space Heating

- Keep hot and cold registers unobstructed.
- Clean or replace furnace filter monthly.
- Service furnace at start of heating season.
- Lower your thermostat to 15°C (59°F) at night or when not at home.
- A comfortable daytime temperature is 22°C (72°F) for most people, higher for infants and seniors.

Hot Water Heating

- Take short showers instead of baths.
- Install low flow shower heads.
- Fix dripping faucets.
- Set hot water tank thermostat below 55°C (131°F).
- Drain your hot water tank every six months.

Transportation

- Install a timer on your block heater.
- Avoid idling vehicles for long periods.
- Check your tire pressure periodically.
- Keep a log book of gas and auto servicing.
- Walk to the local store.
- Car pool at least once a month.
- Use public transit when possible.

Other

- Open curtains and blinds in the morning.
- Keep monthly records to compare utility bills.
- Ensure good attic ventilation.
- Log your own gas meter readings monthly.
- Insulate attic, exterior walls and basement to proper levels.
- Decorate in light colours to brighten rooms.

Score under 25 — There's room for improvement. The money you're spending on wasted energy might be better spent elsewhere. Read through the tips again to see where you can reduce your energy waste.

Score 26-40 — You're a good energy saver, but there's some points that you haven't thought of. Check the list again for hints on wise energy use.

Score over 40 — Congratulations! You're an energy miser. You're well on your way to being Power Smart, and chances are, your family has a little extra money at the end of each month. Keep up the good work!

Leaving the Nest

First-timers often end up lost in the rental maze

by Bill Sass

When the toilet backs up, who're ya gonna call? Katherine Weaver thought it would be nice to call the landlord, especially when the other porcelain appliances started showing signs of temperament. There was only one problem.

"I never met or spoke to the landlord. I had no idea who he was."

It was Weaver's first place of her own 20 years ago as a student in Kingston, Ont., and in a way, it presaged her present job as director of the Edmonton Landlord and Tenant Advisory Board.

"It was sort of an old dilapidated house. The steps leaned one way, the door the other."

"It was subdivided into rooms and full of students. I knew one of the girls renting there and gave her post-dated cheques."

The cheques went to someone who came over to collect them each month—not the landlord. None of the people in the building knew who the landlord was, but "someone knew someone who could get hold of him so he could give permission to fix the plumbing."

She chuckles at the memory—never thinking twice about living in a place that she'd tip-toe by today. But such is the blinkeredness of youth.

"We used to think the place was haunted. We got ice on the back windows in mid-May. The walls were awful, cheap panelling." The panelling was put up to cover walls the police gutted during a drug bust.

Now, dealing with landlords—and renters—is part of her daily life with the advisory board, which acts as a sort of referee and adviser in the sometimes turbulent world of leases and property laws.

First-timers in the rental maze can easily get lost, she said.

"They have great ideas, but nine out of 10 times it works out badly," she said.

Number one on the list is doing an honest and detailed budget before moving out, one that includes everything—income levels are usually so low that an uncounted bus fare, school fee or pack of smokes can turn into a financial disaster.

Whatever's left over is what a person can pay for rent.

"That can be a shock."

Enter the need for roommates, probably the touchiest, most volatile area of renterdom.

"Living with a roommate is sort of like marriage. Those little habits that are so endearing when you're not living together can drive you crazy when you see them every day.

"Don't assume that because you party together, you can live together."

You have to ask a lot of questions, have a good idea about each other's habits, waking hours, cleanliness, chores, food and, above all, the same priority about paying rent.

Having settled accounts, priorities and roommates, it's time to go out and get a place.

Getting A Place

Rule 1.

Look at the place you're going to rent. This isn't as stupid as it sounds. Sometimes a landlord will say "I can't show you the suite now, there are eople there, but I can show you one ust like it across the hall." Don't buy . On moving-in day, you might find e real suite has been used as a land- ll site. You will be unhappy.

Rule 2.

ead the lease. It's a legal document nd it's not easy to change or get out of . Even if the landlord gives you the oot because of your noisy parties, you ay still be liable for certain things. If here are two people on the lease and ne moves out, the remaining body is 00 per cent responsible for rent. Got a ew buddy to come in and share? The andlord will have to approve him/her ust like the original tenants were ap- roved. Don't assume the rent can't be iked during the lease's term (read it). landlord can turf you under certain ircumstances, giving you notice of as ttle as 48 hours to three months. In periodic lease, you have to be given hree months' notice for a rent increase nd you have to give, IN WRITING, a 0-day notice to the landlord if you're oving out.

Rule 3.

et it in writing and get it in detail. Do you get a parking space, storage n the basement? Are the utilities in- luded? What will the landlord do in erms of cleaning and repair before ou move in? If you've agreed to do ome work in exchange for rent, write t down. The most important docu- nent is the moving-in/moving-out re- ort. You and the manager/landlord hould, within 48 hours of your mov- ng in, go over the apartment IN MINUTE DETAIL, writing down every pot on the rug (make a diagram), hip in the wall, hole in the door, nissing shelves or crack in the win- low. Make sure you both sign it.

Rule 4.

f you break it, fix it or get it fixed. ometimes things happen that you nay not be responsible for—like a tile alling off the tub surround. But you re responsible for notifying the man- .ger and not causing further damage y getting the bare area wet.

Rule 5.

Talk to the manager or landlord if you're having problems. Landlords have mortgage payments, too, and they get might irate if their own cheque bounces because your money isn't there to cover it. Most will be un- derstanding. Don't make late rent a habit, however.

Rule 6.

The biggest bugaboo landlords have is noise. Keep it within your walls. You can be turfed if you or your bud- dies make a nuisance of themselves.

Rule 7.

When you leave, you have to leave the place reasonably clean. This is where things usually, if not always, get dicey. Remember that move-in tour you took with the landlord when you moved in? If there is more unfixed damage not covered on that report, expect to have it deducted from your damage deposit. Don't expect to get your deposit back the day you move out. The landlord has 30 days to give you the refund and he or she will usually take it.

Students Fall Easily into Credit Trap

Dear Ann Landers:

I am writing about a problem I hear about every day but rarely see addressed in your column—students with credit card debt.

Credit card companies are sending pre-approved credit cards to high school seniors and college freshmen who have little or no income, believing that parents will pay when the bills come due.

In today's buy-now-pay-later society, it's easy for anyone to get into trouble with credit cards but especially kids who see them as free money—young people who have never had to support themselves. I've talked to students who just throw the bill away when they get it because they can't pay the $1,000 in charges they've run up—and they're still using the card.

Parents need to have frank discussions with their children about credit long before these cards start coming in the mail. Kids need to be told what bad credit can do to them—from not being able to rent an apartment to being denied a first job. Ann, did you know that employers now check credit history and reject applicants with bad credit ratings as poor risks?

Please get the word out, and help graduates get off to a better start.

Benjamin Dover, KLIF Radio, Dallas

Dear Benjamin:

Thank you for a letter that could be the most important assignment my student readers have received this year. The lesson you have laid out could spell disaster if flunked.

The buy-now-pay-later trap can be extremely seductive. It's so tempting. The nightmare begins when you realize you are paying interest on things you bought a long time ago and not getting out of debt.

Smart people pay cash or settle their credit card purchases at the end of every month. It's a lot cheaper in the long run, and you will sleep better at night.

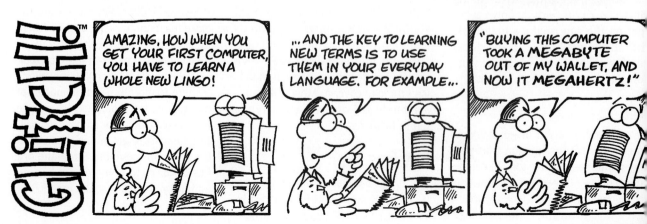

© GLITCH GRAPHIC

Your In-Home Water Audit

Check the box if you already practise these wise water habits.

Kitchen and Laundry

☐ 1. Run your dishwasher only when you have a full load.
Every time you use your dishwasher you use about 120 litres of water.
Every time you use your washing machine you use about 230 litres of water.

☐ 2. Don't let the faucet run while you clean vegetables.
You can serve the same purpose by putting the stopper in the sink and filling it with clean water.

☐ 3. If you wash dishes by hand, don't leave the water running for rinsing.
If you have two sinks, fill one with soapy water and one with rinse water. If you have only one sink, gather all the washed dishes in a dish rack and rinse them with an inexpensive spray device or pour water over the dishes with a pitcher.

☐ 4. Be sure you turn off sink taps completely after use and check to ensure your faucets and pipes do not leak.
Even the smallest drip from a worn washer can waste 50 litres or more a day.

☐ 5. Fill a pitcher with water and keep it in the refrigerator or stock your freezer with ice cubes rather than letting the water run until it gets cold.

Bathroom

☐ 1. Install water-saving shower heads or flow restrictors.
Most shower heads put out 25-50 litres/minute; 15 litres/minute is sufficient for a refreshing shower. Your local hardware or plumbing supply stocks inexpensive water-saving shower heads you can install easily. For even less, you can purchase a small plastic insert to limit flow through your present shower head.

☐ 2. Put two plastic bottles filled with pebbles and water in your toilet tank away from the operating mechanism.
Your toilet is one of your home's biggest water users and can probably flush just as efficiently with less water than it uses now. The bottles may displace as much as 50 litres of water or more a day. It is also a much better idea than a brick in the toilet tank. Bricks can disintegrate and damage plumbing.

☐ 3. Check your toilet for leaks.
A leak in your toilet may be wasting more than 400 litres of water a day. To check, put a little food coloring in your toilet tank. If, without flushing, the coloring begins to appear in the bowl, you have a leak. Adjust or replace the flush valve or call a plumber.

☐ 4. Take shorter showers.
Long, hot showers waste 25-50 litres every unneeded minute. Limit your showers to the time it takes to soap up, wash and rinse.

☐ 5. Turn off the water after wetting your toothbrush.
After you have wet your toothbrush and filled a glass for rinsing your mouth, turn off the tap water.

☐ 6. Rinse your razor in the sink.
Before shaving, partially fill the sink with warm water. This will rinse the blade just as well and use less water.

☐ 7. Stop using your toilet as an ashtray or a wastebasket.
Every time you flush a cigarette butt, facial tissue or other small bit of trash down the toilet, you waste 23 litres of water.

Rules of the Road When Setting Up

Thinking about making the Big Move away from Mom and Dad and Sis and your brother and all the rules about being in, checking in and playing your music?

Here are some pointers from the voices of experience interviewed for this story.

You may think this is a lot to deal with—but remember, an apartment of your own means a sewing room for your dear old mother and you can play your Malignant Nosehair tape over and over and over...and no one will say a word.

Talk to people

This is at the top of the list because it's the most important thing. Despite what you think, you probably don't know a lot of stuff and to get the answers, to protect your interests and get your point across you HAVE TO TALK. I know some people who were afraid to ask a bus driver where his bus was going and usually wound up on the wrong side of the city. Most of the people you'll be dealing with are used to being talked to and answering questions, even landlords and utility clerks. They won't mind it if you ask questions and make reasonable demands. They might think you're strange if you don't.

Deposits and hook-ups

A lot of people get into trouble right from the start because they don't think about start-up costs like damage deposits (usually one month's rent), utility deposits and hook-up fees. If you have no credit rating or a bad one, expect to hand $500 (yes, $500) to the friendly, though untrusting folk at the local telephone company—that's on top of the $55 hook-up charge. If your apartment doesn't come with power and water supplied, you'll need a $65 power and $50 water deposit and must pay $22 and $23.50, respectively, for a hook-up. The good news is that some utility companies don't require a deposit or hook-up charge for gas. Total upfront charges: $703.15, plus damage deposit. You can also try to establish some sort of credit rating before you leave home. This lowers or eliminates some deposit requirements. Maybe mom and dad will co-sign for some of this—maybe they won't.

Think about small stuff

All the things your parents supply now that you don't think about. Got a vacuum cleaner stashed in your closet? Probably not. (A stiff broom works pretty well—but don't forget a dustpan). Towels? Sheets? Pillows? (Tip. Use rags. They can be washed and are cheaper than paper towels).

Start-up costs

Mom and dad buy salt when they run out. The same with pepper and dish detergent. You have to buy things like that ALL AT ONCE, before you have the privilege of replacing them one at a time. Let's see: dish towels and dish cloths, scouring pads, toilet paper toothpaste, cleaners, laundry soap ketchup, marge, garlic powder; sewing stuff, tacks and pins, clothes hangers (I always thought they bred themselves in the closet), Band Aids, aspirin, scissors, some small tools, extension cords batteries. Someone even mentioned shower curtain rings. Scrounge as much as you can from home.

Check your medical, dental and eyeglass coverage

Will your parents' insurance cover you for a while or will you have to make your own payments?

Address changes

Driver's licences, library card, whatever. Sometimes it'll cost you, sometimes it won't. Notify the post office so you get your mail delivered to your house. You'll need a newspaper. Yes, really. If nothing else, it's the cheapest and quickest route you have to job notices and classified sales ads.

Budget, Budget, Budget

Be honest. Be real. Count EVERYTHING, from cigarettes, to bus passes, to laundry, to drinks and movies and food and your pack-a-day chewing gum habit. A wild $30 night on the town can represent 20 percent of your paycheque for a week and wreck your personal economy if you haven't planned for it.

- Add 7 percent. Add provincial tax too, if you have to. Everything, except grocery-bought food, carries a seven per cent federal tax (GST). Some things have it built in. Generally, however, it's $7 on a hundred. It adds up. The good news: If you're a low-income earner, you'll likely get all or part of it back in quarterly instalments from the feds if you're over 19 and IF YOU'VE FILED A TAX RETURN THE PREVIOUS YEAR. Rejoice.

Buy bulk, whenever possible

It's cheaper. If you have friends or relatives in retail, use them to get deals if possible. Shop the larger, warehouse stores. Don't ever do serious grocery shopping in a convenience store. You can't afford it. No one can. Take a bus to stores with good deals and cab home with the goodies. You'll likely still be ahead.

The roommate(s)

When you've subtracted your expenses from your income, you'll know how many roommates you'll need. Pick wisely and ask questions. Get the rules

Your new home is a blank canvas — give it personality!

straight. Hold up your end. Don't sweat the small stuff. If you have to part ways, make it as friendly as possible (this avoids smashing of walls and losses of deposits and personal property). If possible, go to where a prospective roommate lives and look around. Live with them for a week, if you can, to get an idea of what they're like. Ask for references. Write things down.

Check out the banks you deal with

Look at their charges and what they offer. Sometimes they'll freeze an account for up to 30 days while a cheque clears. If you don't have the money in the bank, don't write the cheque. It's VERY expensive to bounce a cheque to save face and the hole just gets deeper. The longer you deal with a bank, the more it trusts you. Bounce enough cheques and some of them will "fire" you as a customer (truth).

Learn to cook, if you don't know how

You don't have to become a master chef, but there is certain basic knowledge about turning raw food into something more-or-less edible.

Newspapers have easy recipes. There are books. Why bother? The $10 you'll spend at the Burger Burp can buy you two, maybe three, meals at home.

Furniture?

Say hello to the second-hand folks and garage sale people. Keep you ear to the ground. Sometimes people will GIVE you furniture if you just take it away. Cultivate a friend with a pickup truck.

Manage your time

It takes more time to live poor. People with more money often spend it to buy the convenience of not having to look or travel around for the bargains. This is where you will learn, without a doubt, that time is money.

Have fun

There'll be bad days and good days. But remember: no bedtime and you can stay out until all hours if you want—unless, of course, you have to get to work or school or to the dentist or store or...welcome to the world of grown-ups.

Live long and prosper.

Power Shopping

by John Bissonnette

Paul and Jane Fields found out recently that buying a major electric appliance can be a challenging experience. The young couple was surprised at the range of models available and the differences between them. They also had questions about the EnerGuide labels which were displayed on virtually every major home appliance they saw.

With the help of Michael Phillips, their local appliance dealer, Paul and Jane quickly learned how to use the EnerGuide label to identify energy-efficient appliances that will save them money.

He explained to them that the EnerGuide label indicates how much energy the appliance consumes. It also shows a scale that can be used to compare the energy efficiency of one appliance to another with the same capacity and features.

"Take, for example, the EnerGuide label on this clothes washer," Michael said. "The scale on the label shows that the most energy-efficient model in this class consumes 643 kilowatt-hours (kWh)[1] of electricity, while the least efficient model consumers 1500 kWh. The most energy-efficient appliance has the lowest kWh rating on the scale and will have the lowest electricity cost."

"So, the further left the arrow — the more efficient the appliance," said Jane.

"Exactly," replied Michael. "Over the lifespan of an appliance, hundreds of dollars can be saved in energy costs simply by buying an energy-efficient model — and that is just for one appliance. The EnerGuide label applies to ranges, refrigerators, freezers, dishwashers, clothes washers and dryers and room air conditioners. Think of the money you'll save by looking to the left of the scale for top energy performers."

Use the "Big Number" to Get the Big Picture!

"So what does this big number in the middle of the label mean?" asked Paul.

"It tells you how much energy in kWh the appliance will use in one year under normal operating conditions," replied Michael. "And it can be used to determine the total energy cost over the life of the appliance — 'the second price tag'."

Michael then took out a paper and pen to show what he meant, using two comparable clothes washers as examples. By multiplying the number on the label by the price of electricity, you can quickly estimate how much it will cost to operate the appliance for one year. Multiply that number by the average life of the appliance and you'll get the "second price tag".

Michael then performed the same calculation for the other clothes washer to illustrate the difference in lifetime energy costs.

"Is the EnerGuide label really a seal of approval, telling us that the appliance is energy efficient?" asked Paul.

"No, it is not," cautioned Michael, offering the following explanation.

"The EnerGuide label signifies only that the appliance meets a minimum level of energy efficiency, which is now regulated by the federal government. The appearance of an EnerGuide label does not necessarily mean that the appliance is a good energy performer. What's important is the location of the arrow on the scale and the appliance's annual energy consumption in kWh. The numbers on the EnerGuide scales are adjusted each year to take into account the introduction of new models and to keep pace with constant improvements in the energy efficiency of household appliances."

The refrigerators built today are nearly three times more efficient than those built 20 years ago. Freezers are twice as efficient, and dishwashers are one and a half times more efficient.

Bonus: Energy Efficiency Helps the Environment!

"Just out of curiosity, why is the government regulating energy efficiency?" asked Jane.

"That's a good question," acknowledged Michael. "The government is trying to eliminate the most inefficient appliances from the market as a way of reducing energy consumption across Canada while helping the environment. Some of the energy we use in Canada is produced by burning fossil fuels, like oil and coal, which generates greenhouse gases and contributes to the global warming trend you have probably been reading and hearing about in the media."

"So energy efficiency will not only save us money, it's good for the environment," concluded Jane. "I like that idea."

To help Paul and Jane compare appliances without having to leave the store, Michael gave them a copy of the 2001 *EnerGuide Appliance Directory*, which contains the EnerGuide ratings for all major electric household appliances imported into Canada or shipped between provinces. He also gave them a copy of the *Consumer's Guide to Buying and Using Energy-Efficient Appliances*.

After reviewing the two booklets and looking at several other clothes washers, Jane and Paul made their decision — they purchased the most energy-efficient model.

Want to Learn More?

Most appliance retailers employ salespeople like Michael Phillips who have received EnerGuide Retailer Training. However, the *EnerGuide Appliance Directory*, the 2001 *EnerGuide Directory of Room Air Conditioner* and the *Consumer's Guide to Buying and Using*

Energy-Efficient Appliances, published by Natural Resources Canada (NRCan), may not always be available through retailers. Information on this subject is also available on the Internet at http://energy-publications.nrcan.gc.ca/index_e.cfm

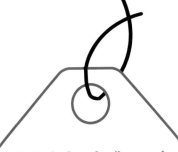

Calculating the "second price tag"

kWh per year from the EnerGuide label x cost of electricity per kWh* x appliance's anticipated life = Second Price Tag

(Use the following general guidelines for appliance life expectancy:

dishwashers — 13 years;

clothes washers — 14 years;

clothes dryers — 18 years;

freezers — 21 years;

ranges — 18 years; and

refrigerators — 17 years.)

*check your electricity bill to get the kWh cost for your region.

Look to the left for the top energy performers

These EnerGuide labelling scales indicate the range of energy consumption for some of the most common classes and sizes of electric household appliances sold in Canada. When purchasing one of these appliances, look for a model where the arrow is as far to the left of the scale as possible.

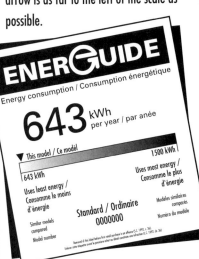

RANGE
715 kWh — 828 kWh

REFRIGERATOR
515 kWh — 762 kWh

CHEST FREEZER
437 kWh — 441 kWh

DISHWASHER
381 kWh — 698 kWh

CLOTHES WASHER
537 kWh — 1000 kWh

CLOTHES DRYER
877 kWh — 950 kWh

[1] One kilowatt hour (kWh) is the amount of electrical energy supplied by one kilowatt over a one hour period. It is the basic unit of measurement for electrical energy. Electricity bills are based in part on the number of kilowatt hours a customer has used during a billing period. For example, using a 100-watt light bulb for 10 hours consumes 1000 watt hours, or one kilowatt hour, of electricity.

HOME AGAIN

by Jeff Holubitsk*

As a tight economy forces more adult children back to the nest, they and their parents are forging new relationships.

Two years ago, Don Kung would never have believed he'd be living back home in his mom and dad's basement.

He though the world was his oyster. He was going off to Montreal to learn the fashion business

But after two years at school, a failed relationship and a fruitless job search, the 26-year-old returned to the nest last June as part of a growing trend of adult children in need.

"There were no jobs for me and I was running out of money at the same time," he says.

"I had to swallow my pride a bit, but I wanted to go back home again for some kind of stability."

One of the first things he realized was that things would never be like they were before. He sat down with his parents and worked out a deal. He'd pay his own way except for rent.

"We basically lead our own lives, and I'm responsible for my own finances," he says.

"I feel we can talk to each other on an equal basis."

When he was younger, Kung liked to party and go out with friends. Now he's intent on saving money to get into engineering at university next fall.

His mother would like to see him date, but after being used to bringing a girlfriend home to his own place, he'd never bring one to his parents' home.

"Now I'm a little more guarded."

"Recognize that life is filled with peaks and valleys and just because you've moved home you are not a failure"

Soon after returning home, Kung went through a brief period of conflict with his dad, who didn't think he was trying hard enough to get a job. That situation was fortunately resolved in August when he found work with a plastic manufacturing company.

His toughest ordeal, though, was with the sense of failure he felt in himself. "I battled that one over and over again, and there are times when I feel down or that I am a failure and quit too easily," he says.

Those are times when he considers packing up and moving back to Montreal.

"But I'm thinking that, since I'm here at home, rather than feeling so remorseful, I think I should take advantage of this time to get into something like engineering."

Cheryl Kalinowski, a counsellor with Catholic Social Services, says moving home is not the brand of a loser.

"I don't think the person is a failure. We all have ups and downs in our lives," she says of the adult children sometimes called boomerang kids.

Although no statistics cover kids going home or why they do, Kalinowski has detected an increase.

"I'd have to say I've seen more in my own practice in the past year," she says. Causes often relate to tough times and changing economy.

"A very healthy way of looking at it is to be honest and say this is my situation right now."

When the big move comes, often overnight without much time to think about it, both parents and adult kids must discuss their new roles.

Moms and dads will always be parents. They also have to realize where their responsibilities to their children begin and end, says Kalinowski.

"This is your child, but the relationship is different."

And adult children have to understand they can't relive the carefree lives of a young kid.

"Some people are always in that role around their parents," Kalinowski says of those who rely on their parents instead of acting independently.

"They never make that transition to having an adult-to-adult relationship, so that one is not in a one-up position."

Like it or not, kids who move home may be imposing on their parents, even when they are welcome.

Social matters have to be discussed. Can friends come in? How long can they stay? Can someone stay overnight?

"These are things where you have to use some common sense and you have to talk about them ahead of time."

Sometimes moving back home works, and other times it doesn't, says Cheryl Kalinowski of Catholic Social Services.

Both parents and their kids have to take stock of their relationships - both today and back when they first parted.

Did the teenager leave in a huff, or was leaving natural and positive?

Here are some things Kalinowski suggests people consider before agreeing to the big move:

- Do parents and children regard each other as adults or is one still the parent and the other the child? Before any living arrangements can work, both parties must see each other as equals to avoid the one-upmanship which can ensue.

- Discuss and arrive at a mutually agreed contract before the move home is made. Discuss privacy, habits, morals, beliefs, participation in the home and monetary issues. Even such little things as payment for long distance calls can scuttle a parent-older child relationship. There should be a periodic review of the contract agreed upon in advance.

- Emphasis needs to be placed on the difference between now and when the adult child previously lived at home. Base this on changes in both parents' and child's lives.

- Be aware and pay attention to when you get caught up in the old parent-child roles.

- Don't take advantage of the situation. Both parties must continue to pull their weight.

- Recognize that the anger you show towards your parent may really be anger you are feeling about your situation. If anger has become a problem, see a therapist or join an anger management group to work on your issues.

- Be flexible and willing to make changes if your contract isn't working.

- Set aside time for your personal interests. All relationships require individual time as well as time together.

- Recognize that life is filled with peaks and valleys and just because you've moved home you are not a failure.

- A sense of humour is necessary to make any relationship work - including one with your parents.

The Price of
Part-Time Pay

by Deborah Jones

Last spring, when classes ended for the day at Brookswood Secondary School in Langley, B.C., 19-year-old Rebecca Taylor went straight to work as a lifeguard, joining thousands of her teenage peers across Canada who trundle off after school to their part-time jobs slinging burgers or fitting shoes. Many of them clock up to 20 hours or more a week to top up their allowances, save for university or supplement the family income.

Until a few years ago, many teens only worked during the summer. Now, more than 36 percent of Canadian students ages 15 to 19 earn money after school, reports Statistics Canada. At another Langley high school, D.W. Poppy Secondary School, about 70 percent of students in Grades 10 to 12 hold jobs. While juggling a job and schoolwork can motivate teens to manage time wisely and perform better overall, educators fear that too many kids are swapping their long-term prospects for temporary positions. Says Brookswood's principal, Cam Gesy, "School should be a full-time job, or almost a full-time job, because of the intense competition for postsecondary placements."

What distinguishes a positive working experience from a drain on time and energy? The key, says Gesy, is how organized the student is, and more important, how many hours he or she works each week. Gesy warns that working more than 15 hours a week may compromise school performance.

In today's global job market, Canadian kids face stiff competition from students from other countries. In Japan, for example, kids spend their extra time studying at cram school instead of squandering their valuable learning time flipping burgers. But controlling the time teens put in at their jobs can be a challenge. When students try to cut back on their hours, employers often pressure them. "This is especially true during sale time and in heavy commercial periods like Mother's Day, which is when the students are writing exams," Gesy says.

Parents can help by sending clear signals that school comes first. In Rebecca Taylor's case, she wasn't allowed to get a part-time job until her last year in high school. "My friends thought I was spoiled," she says. Her mother thinks otherwise. "She needed time to do her homework and socialize," explains Susan Taylor, who works in a municipal land-title office. The Taylors' focus on school paid off when Rebecca won a $10,000 scholarship to go to the University of British Columbia. And, as Susan Taylor sees it, too many teens work for the wrong reasons. "They have to learn what is more important — and designer jeans aren't that important."

Tips for Teens

Employers often demand the same level of commitment from diligent teens that they would from adults. D.W. Poppy Secondary School in Langley, B.C., has developed strategies to help kids cope. Molly Payne, head counselor, offers the following tips:

- Ask yourself if you really need the job. Why are you working and where is the job leading? Where is school leading?

- Tell your boss when you prefer to work, when you can work if necessary and when you absolutely cannot work — well in advance. "Don't suddenly announce that you have a test on the same day as your shift," says Payne.

- If you're in a situation you truly can't handle, ask your parents to step in and become involved in any discussions.

- When problems arise, ask your supervisor for a convenient time to talk things over.

Goal Setting

by Rosalie Pedersen

Setting goals is a lifetime process. While some goals fall into place, others need some planning.

1. Write down everything you would like to have and do in life (including fun things) on a piece of paper. Let your imagination go wild!
2. Number them in order of importance.
3. Decide how much time you need for each goal — one, two or five years.
4. Plan a few steps that you know you can accomplish each day.
5. Review your goals and make changes when you feel you need to.
6. Celebrate each accomplishment — we knew you could do it!

A Financial Plan Will Help

The fist step towards creating a financial plan is knowing your goals. Many people don'trealize that a plan is critical if you want to reach those financial goals. This is a big job and there are many articles here to help you. Writing a personal financial plan can be a surprisingly simple process, although it will take a few hours.

Knowing your goals will help you determine what money you need when. The next step is seeing if you can make that money available. Chances are, you are not going to be able to instantly earn the money for some of your goals, so you need to start saving. And what are you going to do with your savings, to help them grow? Consider investing.

These are the basic components. There are books, software programs, Internet groups and financial institutions that can give you more information and provide tables and spreadsheets for you to work out the details.

Shattering Those

by Fran Kimmel

What stops us from doing all the things we want to do? Often, it's because we tell ourselves we can't. We feed ourselves messages like "I'm too awkward" or "I'm not smart enough" or "I'll look like an idiot" or....

These messages are called blocks. Blocks are not real, they're imagined. And as we start listening to them — and believing them — they can take over a whole lot of things. Like our lives.

Think of all the would-be-scientists, Olympic contenders and rock stars out there who talked themselves out of chasing their dream in precisely this way.

Do negative thoughts creep in and crack holes in your confidence? If the answer is yes, you may need to bulldoze those mental blocks.

Mental Blocks

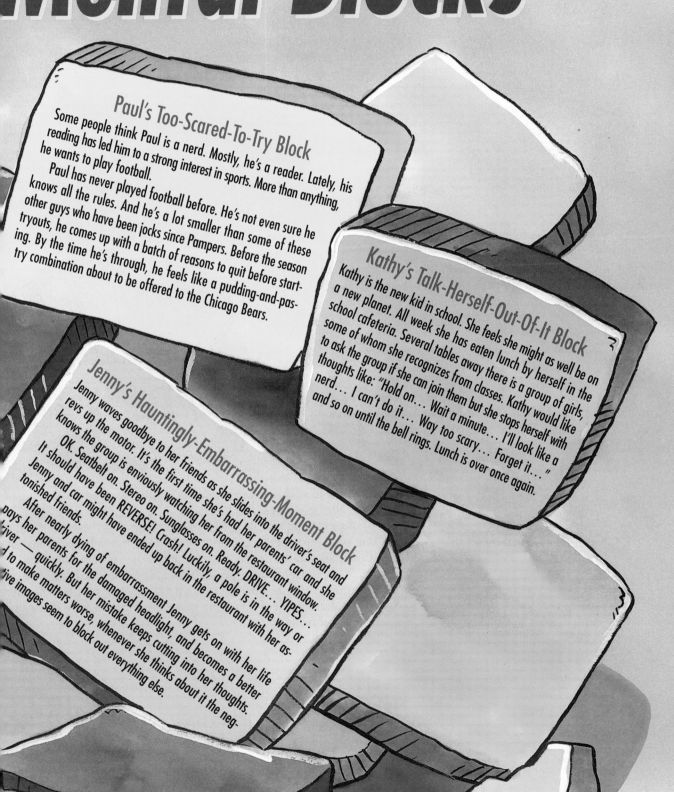

Paul's Too-Scared-To-Try Block

Some people think Paul is a nerd. Mostly, he's a reader. Lately, his reading has led him to a strong interest in sports. More than anything, he wants to play football.

Paul has never played football before. He's not even sure he knows all the rules. And he's a lot smaller than some of these other guys who have been jocks since Pampers. Before the season tryouts, he comes up with a batch of reasons to quit before starting. By the time he's through, he feels like a pudding-and-pastry combination about to be offered to the Chicago Bears.

Kathy's Talk-Herself-Out-Of-It Block

Kathy is the new kid in school. She feels she might as well be on a new planet. All week she has eaten lunch by herself in the school cafeteria. Several tables away there is a group of girls, some of whom she recognizes from classes. Kathy would like to ask the group if she can join them but she stops herself with thoughts like: "Hold on… Wait a minute… I'll look like a nerd… I can't do it… Way too scary… Forget it…" and so on until the bell rings. Lunch is over once again.

Jenny's Hauntingly-Embarrassing-Moment Block

Jenny waves goodbye to her friends as she slides into the driver's seat and revs up the motor. It's the first time she's had her parents' car and she knows the group is enviously watching her from the restaurant window.

OK. Seatbelt on. Stereo on. Sunglasses on. Ready. DRIVE… YIPES… It should have been REVERSE! Crash! Luckily, a pole is in the way or Jenny and car might have ended up back in the restaurant with her astonished friends.

After nearly dying of embarrassment Jenny gets on with her life — she pays her parents for the damaged headlight, and becomes a better driver — quickly. But her mistake keeps cutting into her thoughts. And to make matters worse, whenever she thinks about it the negative images seem to block out everything else.

Bulldozer #1

Think of something you have always wanted to do. Take up a new sport? Try out for a part in a school play? Ask someone for a date? Write your private passion at the top of a sheet of paper.

Now think of the blocks. Think of all the reasons stopping you and write them down. Paul's page might have looked like this:

- I want to try out for the football team but:
- I'm too old to start now.
- I don't know the rules.
- The guys are going to kill me.
- I'll break both legs the first time out.
- I'll never be any good.
- I'm too small.
- They're all going to laugh.

The next step is to review your list and blast away at everything that is not real. (If arguing with yourself seems ridiculous, you may want to pull in a friend for this part.) Bulldoze through the imagined stuff so that you can use your energy to tackle the real issues — like what is the best way to learn the rules of football.

You want to do something, but it's just too scary. Don't give up. Instead, think of all the most unbelievably awful things that could happen if you were to go ahead. (You're thinking of them anyway, so you might as well make an exercise out of it — right?)

Kathy in the cafeteria might have thought:

- I'll get to their table and forget my name.
- All my clothes will fall off.
- I'll faint and land in my taco chips.
- They'll see me coming, scream and run away.

Enough. Enough. Now bring yourself back to reality, have a laugh and be relieved that nothing like that will happen. For Kathy, at worst, it might have been awkward to think of things to say. That's nothing compared to the nightmare she's been through. She might as well go for it. You might too.

Bulldozer #2

Bulldozer #3

This one is great when something is bugging you and just won't quit. Like after Jenny's car accident.

Let's say you have dealt with your problem in the best way possible, but you keep worrying about it anyway. Next time it happens, imagine this problem takes up space in your mind. Then go into your mind, remove the thought, and replace it with the most terrific image you can conjure up. Use the same image each time so it starts to become automatic, and soon you will control those nagging thoughts — instead of them controlling you.

What became of this troubled trio?

Paul accepted the position of football trainer. Kathy was invited to join that same group of girls the next day. And Jenny now laughs at the tale of her first glass-shattering experience.

Different teens. Different situations. But the same painful process.

Paul, Kathy and Jenny may have found life easier if they had known ways to get past their own negative messages. Next time you're faced with a battle of the blocks, why not plan on a little bulldozing?

A Holiday Credit Saver

Reduce your holiday spending debt with smart credit choices

by Joanne Thomas Yaccato

Last year, while wiping out a department store's toy inventory shopping for Kate's first Christmas, the phrase "holiday cards" took on a whole new meaning for me. "And how will you be paying today?" the salesclerk asked. "What do you take?" I asked from behind Muttsy the giant stuffed dog. "Our store card, American Express, Visa, MasterCard, debit card, cheque with a credit card and driver's licence." She didn't mention cash, though I think they'd have taken that too.

With that many payment options — and with personal debt at an all-time high — how can you ensure you make smart use of your "holiday cards"? The only real solution: self-discipline and a clear understanding of what credit options best match your spending style.

Credit Where It's Due

Credit cards give you access to credit through a financial institution, department store or gas company. Store and gas cards charge stratospheric annual interest rates in the range of 24 to 30 percent. Banks or trust companies charge between 14 and 18 percent for standard cards; 6 to 13 for low-rate option cards. Watch out for annual fees: depending on your balance, the fee may end up costing you more than a card with a higher interest rate but no fee. (For instance, on an outstanding balance of $1,500, a card with an interest rate of 13.5 percent with a $60 annual fee ends up costing you the same as a no-fee card at 17.5 percent.) Grace period — the time from statement date until they apply interest charges — is usually 21 days. You can carry a balance indefinitely as long as you make the minimum monthly payments and don't exceed your limit.

Charge cards such as American Express are for the financially responsible only, since they have no preset spending limit and require payment in full each month. Annual fees range from $55 to $250. The grace period is usually 30 days, but the late penalties are stiff: equal to 30 percent annually.

Value-added cards may be credit or charge cards, with extra features such as airline or merchandise points, buyer's insurance, travel insurance and more. Often they have an annual fee: make sure the extra features are worth it.

With debit cards, you can't spend what you don't have. The cards are used to withdraw funds directly from your account at the point of purchase.

If you insist on using a credit card, keep just one low-rate card or a charge card that you must pay off each month.

Transaction fees range from 20 cents to 50 cents, but may be waived depending on your account balance and type.

What Should You Use?

If you're still paying for holiday gifts while sunbathing in August, caving in to impulse credit purchases and rationalizing credit-spending with thoughts like, "If I buy this gold-plated weed whacker for Mom, I'll get enough points to get myself that tin-plated shovel for free," you could be heading to credit-card hell.

So what should you do? The simple fact is credit may not be for you right now. The smart thing would be to cancel the cards and pay off the debt with a line of credit or consolidation loan. Try (and here's where the self-discipline comes in) switching to a debit card. If you insist on using a credit card, keep just one low-rate card or a charge card that you must pay off each month. One option for next year: start making monthly contributions to a Canada Savings Bond when they come around in October so that the following December, you can shop with cash.

If you generally pay off balances within a couple of months, then you're in the responsible-user realm. You can feel comfortable using most of the card options available, but if you consistently take a couple of months to pay off balances, low-rate cards are your best bet.

And then there's the person the rest of us strive to be: the credit puritan who pays off cards in full each month. You are safe with any of the options, but the value-added card is your best bet. That way, you finance your purchases for 21 days on the financial institution's dime, while also earning points for tin shovels and trips to Buffalo, N.Y.

The bottom line? Match proper credit options to your lifestyle and spending habits and it will go a long way toward ensuring the season is as it should be: merry.

Charge!

❄ The average Canadian wallet contains 2.6 credit cards

❄ In 2002 Canadians spent $110 billion on MasterCard and Visa alone.

❄ Between 1990 and 2001, outstanding balances on credit cards have grown from $11 billion to $34 billion.

❄ 54 percent of Canadians pay off their Visa or MasterCard in full each month.

Time
there's never enough

Although undoubtedly many Canadians have always felt that they didn't have enough time, those sentiments have increased greatly in recent years.

✦ The contributions of technology have accelerated expectations about quality and have decimated time-lines.

✦ Fax machines and E-mail, laptops and software, portable printers, cellular phones and PDAs have taken away our hiding places and our excuses for not producing immediate turnarounds.

Asked about trends over the past five years:

✦ 7 in 10 women and men say that "the general pace of life" has been increasing, as have the demands on their time;

✦ close to the same number report having less time for themselves; and

✦ 6 in 10 say there's been a decrease in the time they have to do the things they want.

Those levels, incidentally, are slightly below those 5 years ago, despite our perception that, time-wise, things are worse.

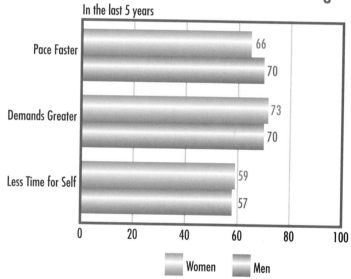

Perception of Time-Related Changes
In the last 5 years

	Women	Men
Pace Faster	66	70
Demands Greater	73	70
Less Time for Self	59	57

For Better or For Worse

FOR BETTER OR FOR WORSE © UNITED PRESS INTERNATIONAL. Reprinted with permission.

The basics of
INVESTING

There is a fine line between saving and investing. Putting money in a jar, tin, or sock is saving. When you put it into a bank savings account, you are investing. You are getting paid interest for the money you have invested in that bank.

Investing your money is putting it to work for you. You can choose to put money in a chequing account. Keep in mind that some chequing accounts pay no interest; some accounts pay a very low interest rate. This type of account is for keeping the money you need on a day-to-day or week-to-week basis. Any excess in this account can be transferred to a savings account, also known as a deposit account, which pays a higher interest rate.

Even when interest rates in the country are really low, your money makes money when it sits in some type of deposit account. The interest rates for these deposit accounts are usually posted in the bank (or you can find out the current interest rate by asking someone in the bank). Some deposit accounts pay a higher interest rate, often based on the amount of money in the account. Use your deposit account for irregular expenses such as saving for Christmas gifts, insurance, and unexpected expenses such a car repairs, for short term goals, or for saving small amounts of money until you have enough to invest in something else that will earn you more interest.

Other investments which usually pay a higher interest but have a very low risk include Canada Savings Bonds. These are issued each year by the Canadian government through the Bank of Canada. They can be purchased in amounts as low as $100. and are basically risk-free. They can be cashed in at any time for the amount they cost you, known as their "face value". However, the point of having CSBs is to leave them to earn interest, therefore making your money work for you. These days you can buy Canada Savings Bonds which mature in ten years, letting your interest work for you, especially if you choose to have compound interest paid on the bonds until they mature (that's when you can cash them in and get the total amount of interest due to you).

There are many other types of low-risk investments. Term deposits and GICs (Guaranteed Investment Certificates) are sold by financial institutions. They are set for a certain term, a certain length of time, and promise to earn a set amount of interest. Some are redeemable, which means you can cash them in at any time. Some are not redeemable until the term is up; these usually earn a higher rate of interest.

As you move up the Pyramid of Relative Investment Risk, you take a higher risk but you have a chance of greater return on your money. It is important to realize that all investments have some degree of risk, increasing as you move up the Pyramid.

Finding and choosing a good investment is not as simple as getting a "hot tip". While you can get good advice from some people around you, you also need to consider the Pyramid and your comfort zone (see p. 92), sometimes known as your "sleeping point" - the point at which you have enough money invested and are not worried about the amount. You also need to have the funds to invest.

Pyramid of Relative Risk

commodity futures, collectibles, speculative common stocks and bonds, security options

real estate investments, limited partnerships

growth shares, growth mutual funds

balanced mutual funds, blue chip common stocks

Guaranteed Investment Certificates (GICs), bonds, preferred shares, income-bond mutual funds, money market accounts

insured chequing and savings accounts, term deposits, treasury bills, Canada Savings Bonds, interest-bearing bank accounts

surrender value of life insurance, other insurance, pension fund, clear title of residence, conservatively invested retirement savings, emergency fund

Highest Risk

Lowest Risk

Note: This is general information. Items on the pyramid can change in level of risk, depending on economic conditions.

Investment Guidelines

You can actually begin to invest with very little money, but there are some guidelines you should follow:

- look at your budget and your spending habits. Is there a place you can reduce your spending and not affect your lifestyle too much? Your saving habits (paying yourself first) means that you will have some funds to place in a low risk investment.

- Remember that good starting investments are the low-risk investments such as term deposits and GICs which are issued by financial institutions (banks, trust companies, credit unions) for a certain period of time, cannot be redeemed before that time, and usually pay a higher interest than a deposit account.

- Use the skills and resources of stockbrokers - their business is to understand the stock market

- Don't buy any investment that you don't understand. Ask questions; if you still don't understand, don't buy. (Remember, you should be reading lots so that your understanding of the process is always increasing.)

- If you can't give a couple of good reasons for buying a stock, don't buy it. Good reasons mean that you have some understanding of what you are buying.

- Don't invest in anything that worries you. Investments should not keep you awake at night. Buy quality stocks, "blue chip" stocks.

- Be patient. If you purchase good quality stocks, they are likely to increase over time, but not on a daily basis. Check the stock pages in the paper if you want but don't worry about day-to-day fluctuations (changes in value).

- Keep good files. All those papers and receipts are an important part of the process of investing.

- Make investing part of your financial plan and then stick to it.

FAQ Investing

- Liquid assets are those which can give you funds immediately. Cash is a liquid asset. So are deposit accounts.

- The trick to investing wisely is to read, read, read. Read basic books on how the stock market works and basic books about mutual funds and other forms of investments.

- Ask your family and friends about how they invest for the future.

- Always save some amount, no matter how small, and bank it every week.

- Don't put all your investments in one place. Keep some money in a savings account, buy a Canada Saving Bond or a term deposit or some shares in a mutual fund. You should have a combination of types of investments; this is called diversification of investments.

- RRSPs - Registered Retirement Savings Plans - are a different type of investment. These are government-approved plans that are tax-sheltered (you don't pay taxes on the interest you earn on them) until you withdraw the money. They are designed to be very long term investments for use when you retire

Tips for Smart
Catalogue Shopping

by Terry Brodie

Whether it's a snuggly quilt or a guitar-shaped toilet seat that has you reaching for an order form, it pays to be a smart catalogue shopper. How to make the most of the experience?

Here are some tips culled from Donna Krampf, director of consumer public relations for the New York-based Direct Marketing Association, and Leila and Elie Albala, co-publishers of the *Catalogue of Canadian Catalogues* (P.O. Box 203, Chambly, Que., J3L 4B3, phone 514-658-6205):

◉ Before you ever place an order, read the catalogue's customer service section. Usually located near the order form, it offers a wealth of shopping information, ranging from sizing charts and satisfaction and return/exchange policies to shipping and handling and tax charges.

◉ To ensure accurate fit, take precise body measurements and compare them against the sizing charts in catalogues. Also ask customer service representatives about how the clothing fits: whether it's tailored or oversized, for example. Another gauge of how clothing will fit: ask what size the model in the catalogue's photo is wearing. When it comes to non-clothing items, check the ad copy for specific dimensions.

◉ To gauge quality and colour, also carefully read catalogue copy for descriptions. And talk to service reps. "Very often, they have the products right in front of them and are taught about them," Ms. Krampf says. You can also ask them to match up items: Does the blue in one piece of clothing seem close to another, for instance? When it comes to clothing, furniture or other material-based merchandise, ask for fabric swatches or wood chips before ordering.

◉ Find out about product warranties up-front; you can often ask for copies before you make any purchases.

◉ Ask specific questions about a company's return policies. They may allow exchanges or credit only or provide refunds. They may accept merchandise back only for specified reasons or have unconditional returns. Be aware that some items, like music or software that can be duplicated, or merchandise that has been monogrammed or otherwise customized, may not be returnable.

There may also be time limits on returns, typically 10 to 30 days, although some companies offer life-time guarantees: cataloguer L.L. Bean recently took back a 45-year old pair of duck boots for resoling, Ms. Krampf says. In addition, check whether the company will cover the costs of returning merchandise.

◉ Find out about all charges, including shipping, handling and taxes, beforehand. Many shipping charges are based on a sliding scale, not on how many items you order but total price. In Canada, add provincial sales tax and GST; in the United States, sales taxes vary by state.

When ordering from U.S. catalogues, find out about currency exchanges, shipping charges and how you have to pay. And ask what companies will cover. Some U.S. cataloguers will pay the mandatory $5 processing fee for orders over $20 and/or duties when Canadians buy south of the border, Ms. Albala says.

◉ Always keep a record of your order, including the name of the company, phone, location, items ordered, sizes, prices, colours, the date the order was placed and how you paid for it, and any confirmation numbers in case you run into problems or items are lost in the mail.

◉ Shopping by fax is becoming more popular — and smart. The company gets your order faster and you have a record of the original order.

SHOPPING ON-LINE

When you shop on-line, you take the same precautions as you do when you shop in the off-line world. Before you enter personal information on a Web site, or make a purchase on-line, here are a few tips:

1. Deal with companies you know by reputation or experience. If you aren't familiar with the company, find out where they are based, and what their policies are on privacy and security. Do not do business with a company that doesn't list an address or phone number on its Web site.

2. Look for a privacy policy. Be sure that you are comfortable with how the company collects, protects and uses your personal information before submitting any details. Responsible marketers have an "opt-out" policy, which allows you to choose whether your information is shared with third parties.

3. Make sure transactions are secure. Do not enter any financial information if you see an open padlock symbol on your Internet browser. This means that the transaction is not secure and could be intercepted by a third party. When the key is complete or the padlock is locked, your browser is indicating a secure transaction. Do not send confidential information by e-mail—they are not secure.

4. Check for endorsement by an association or a quality assurance program. There are several "seals of approval" for Web sites. For example, the Canadian Marketing Association member logo signifies a company that abides by the CMA Code of Ethics and Standards of Practice, which includes a comprehensive privacy policy and a section on responsible Internet marketing.

5. Read the fine print before you buy. Make sure you understand all contractual information before you buy, including the policy on fulfillment, returns, warranties, etc.

6. Avoid spam by being careful about disclosing your e-mail address. Check a company's privacy policy to find out whether your e-mail address could be shared with other companies.

Adapted from: http//www.the-cma.org/ (From the Canadian Marketing Association [CMA])

◎ Ask about delivery dates and shipping options. In the United States, orders must by law be delivered within 30 days unless otherwise specified. In Canada, expect most orders within four weeks.

◎ Never send cash by mail; better to pay by cheque, money order or credit card.

◎ Money-saving tips: Many catalogues contain clearance sections; look for their deals. You should also compare prices in different catalogues that carry the same kinds of wares. And you'll save both time and shipping costs by having gifts delivered directly to their recipients.

◎ Take advantage of free services. Some cataloguers, for instance, offer personal shoppers at no extra charge; some provide speedier delivery for regular delivery charges; and registries are increasingly common.

◎ Always hold on to your receipt and merchandise packaging until you're sure you're satisfied. Some companies won't accept returns without one or both.

◎ If you run into problems, don't hesitate to complain. Start with the company itself; if that gets you nowhere, turn to the direct-mail associations, better business bureaus and government agencies.

You've Got Clout

by Stuart Slayen

Sometimes you probably feel that your parents and teachers aren't paying attention to your needs. And there are times when you feel that your friends and classmates are neglecting you.

But there is one group of people out there that pays attention to every move you make and tries to respond to your every taste, need and desire.

That group is Canada's marketers. The good ones reach out to Canada's teens. They can't afford not to.

Colgate Palmolive, the parent company of Mennen, Speed Stick, Lady Speed Stick and Teen Spirit products, is recognized as a leader in reaching youth across North America. Ian Smith, brand manager for Teen Spirit, estimates that up to 40 per cent of his brand's budget is spent on advertising.

Smith says that there are more than 1.1 million females between the ages of 11 and 16 in Canada. This age group spends around $3.3 billion a year on products for themselves. About $660 million of this is spent on health and beauty products. The numbers did not shrink even during the '90s recession. In fact, says Smith, they continued to grow.

Reaching Canada's youth is a constant challenge. "Teens as a group are much more difficult to reach (than other age groups)," says Smith.

Teen Spirit is advertised in print

(like *What! A Magazine*), on television (MuchMusic and YTV) and in buses. The strategy has been successful as surveys show that over 80 per cent of Canadian teens are familiar with the Teen Spirit product and 30 per cent of females have tried it.

While placing the right ads in the right places is important, even more crucial to corporate Canada is providing the products you want.

Mennen's extensive research showed that young men were satisfied using traditional Mennen men's products while young women had specific interests in underarm products more geared toward their lifestyles.

"Young women's number one concern was wetness protection," says Smith. "They were also more interested in fragrance than older women."

Mennen took their survey results and created Teen Spirit in 1992. Teen Spirit contains allontoin, a special skin conditioning ingredient designed to prevent skin irritation and it also pro-

"What better way to project a product as cool than association with something or someone which is already cool to the teen consumer?"

motes cell regeneration. Part of the fragrance is stored in tiny micro-capsules, and released as activity increases. This was designed to suit the active teen lifestyle.

Even the different Teen Spirit fragrances were specially formulated to suit the teen market. In fact, the fragrance names, Baby Powder Soft, Romantic Rose, California Breeze and Caribbean Cool, were selected by Canadian teens.

You're Being Studied

Believe it or not, corporate marketers and their advertising agencies spend hours and dollars researching and dis-

cussing what young Canadians want.

In 1991, a major conference was held in Toronto where chief marketing professionals gathered to discuss the teen market.

Glenn Wakefield, the advertising manager for Nike Canada, told the conference that Nike tried to portray itself as a cool product.

"What better way to project a product as cool than association with something or someone which is already cool to the teen consumer," he said.

That philosophy has led Nike to include such popular athletes as Michael Jordan and Andre Agassi in their advertising.

Bernard Gorecki and Barbara Gollert from Levi Strauss Canada pre-

sented research findings to the conference including the conclusion that "Canadian youth select their clothing to express something about their attitude towards the world around them. The role of clothing goes beyond the expressions of an attitude — it's part of feeling good about themselves and coping in relationships with others."

Canadian marketers and advertisers have the challenge of coping in their relationships with Canadian teens. As Ian Smith points out, "the teen market is constantly turning over."

The key, says Smith, is conducting research and "staying in touch with what the consumer wants."

The Pleasure is Mutual

You can earn big in mutual funds if you know what you want

by Joanne Thomas Yaccato

What's mutual about it?

Mutual funds were invented to allow the average Jane to benefit from big-dollar investments (stocks, real estate, precious metals, the economy of Japan) usually reserved for big-dollar investors. For as little as $50 a month or a lump-sum deposit of $500, you too can own stock in Bell Canada, Xerox Canada or Noranda. The payoff depends largely on your tolerance for risk.

Are you the roller-coaster type?

Simply put, mutual funds let you share the risk of investment with other investors, and share the rewards of bulk buying. But the potential for gain comes with an equal and opposite potential for loss.

A lot depends on your time line. If you just want a short-term parking place for your cash, a safe choice is *money market funds*. These funds buy mainly risk-free jumbo term deposits, GICs and treasury bills: you get slightly higher interest rates than are available to individuals, but you can likely expect to earn only about 5 to 6 percent over the long term.

If you are 35 and saving for your retirement 30 years down the road, *equity funds* (which invest mainly in stock-market securities) could be your answer, because you can afford to take short-term risks and wait for long-term rewards. You do have to be willing and able to hang on through the stock market's stomach-churning highs and low. Equity funds usually need seven to 10 years to do their best work. Stocks have historically outperformed guaranteed investments

and left evil inflation in the dust. You can expect 10 to 12 percent over the long term with a consistently producing fund. Buy low - think of the fund as being on sale.

If you're prone to lying awake at night wondering what is happening to your hard-earned cash, check out *balanced funds*. They invest in bonds and cash, as well as stocks, and therefore avoid the worst stock-market lows and more exhilarating highs. The growth potential isn't as great as with a pure equity fund, but balanced funds potentially provide money for today as well as for down the road.

If it's hot, it's not

Regardless of your goal, age or financial lot in life, remember this: with mutual funds, there are no guarantees. You can and should find out how a fund, or type of fund, has performed in the past. But you never can know for sure how it will perform in the future.

That's one reason you should not be lured by the spectacular rates of return attached to some specialty funds. Such funds can earn returns of 30, 60 or even 100 percent, but it's impossible to maintain those stratospheric conditions from year to year, and often, when the bottom falls out, it falls out big.

When your neighbour tells you about the latest hot fund she's in, you've already missed the boat. The time to buy a mutual fund is when it's on the way up, not when it's waiting for a fall. A well-chosen financial adviser will show you a fund that has performed consistently in the middle range of performance, rather than at the top or bottom of the market.

The moment of choice

What? You mean out of the measly 1,200 or so mutual funds available in Canada you don't know which to pick? The choice is wide, so you must make it carefully. Educate yourself on the basics: read the relevant section of your favourite financial-planning book and ask for advice from more than one financial expert.

When you've narrowed down your choice, carefully read the prospectus of any fund you are interested in. It will give you details about the securities the fund invests in, and information about the fund's long-term track record.

Highest Risk

Specialty and sector funds

International funds

U.S. equity funds

Real estate funds

Canadian equity funds

Dividend funds

Balanced funds

Bond funds

Mortgage funds

Lowest risk

Money market funds

If your mutual fund type is high risk, your potential reward is high too. But so is the potential for loss.

Reboot Your Home Office

Home offices and game rooms are great, but all that electronic equipment can put extra punch into your electricity bill. How much "extra" depends on the equipment you buy and how you use it. Here's a list of 10 ways to cut down on needless energy use *without* cramping your style. Drum roll, please...

1 Turn equipment off when you're not using it. If your computer takes a while to reboot, take advantage of the time to tidy up the office. And if you have to keep your computer on to receive faxes, switching to "hibernate" mode is an easy way to save energy.

2 Plan for the future when you buy a computer. If you get a notebook, make sure the LCD screen and hard drive are large enough, because you won't be able to replace them with something bigger, as you can with a desktop.

3 If you're buying a printer, ask yourself if you really need a laser printer. Inkjet machines are excellent for home use, and much cheaper if not heavily used. Black and white printers are the most efficient of all. Also, consider getting a printer or copier that can print on both sides of the paper.

4 Think about getting a unit that incorporates a printer, fax, scanner, and copier. If you can't afford a "multifunction," get a printer that can be upgraded with attachments.

Make sure the energy-saver option on your computer is turned on. Computers with the "Power Smart Saves" or "Energy Star" labels can save you money in electricity costs when this option is activated.

5 Cut down on paper use. Do you need to send a cover sheet with every fax? Try to store documents electronically — this saves electricity, paper and space.

6 Use your fax modem. It's more energy efficient than a fax machine, and you'll save on paper and stamps.

7 Internal modems and drives come with your computer these days. This saves energy as well as desk space. If you use external drives or modems, plug them into a switched power bar. This lets you turn off all the equipment at once.

8 Plug video games and other electronic gear into a switched power bar. Use the switch on the power bar to turn this equipment off. If you don't the AC/DC converters will use electricity continuously, giving off heat in the process.

9 Because electronic equipment generates some heat, choose the location of your home office or game room carefully. Putting equipment in an attic room, for example, means you may need an air conditioner to keep the room cool in the summer. For more information, NRCan has published the *Guide to Energy-Efficient Office Equipment.* To order a free copy, call 1-800-387-2000.

Know Where Your Power Goes

In most homes, kitchen appliances use more than 50% of all household electricity. That's because of high wattage equipment, like stoves — and appliances which operate all the time, like your refrigerator. But there are easy ways to reduce your household power costs.

It's Common Sense — Not Sacrifice!

Saving power doesn't mean you need to sit "in the dark". Being Power Smart® isn't about sacrifices — it's about efficiency and common sense.

With little effort, many people can reduce their power bills by over 20% — by carefully choosing the kinds of electrical products they buy — and the way they use electricity.

In the Kitchen...

- Always place your refrigerator and freezer away from heat sources like your range, dishwasher, direct sunlight, and heat vents.
- Keep the fridge at 3˚C and the freezer at -18˚C for better efficiency and food safety.
- If you're cooking small amounts of food, use small appliances like a microwave or toaster oven.

- Make sure your dishwasher is full before you run it through. For even more savings, only use the wash cycle and let the dishes drip dry.
- A second fridge can cost $14 a month, especially older models. Do you really need the extra cold storage?

Around the house...

- If you're not using it, turn it off! That means lights, TV, radios, computers — just turning off your computer overnight can save $4 a month.

- Use the cold water rinse in your laundry — it saves energy and reduces wrinkles. And always wash with full loads.
- Reduced use of a furnace fan can save $15 a month. In summer, only run the fan for a few hours during the coolest part of the day to circulate air throughout the house. In colder months, set the fan to cycle when heat is needed.
- Only use an electric heater until the chill is gone from a room. Using an electric heater — even a small ceramic one — can cost up to $40 a month just to heat one room.

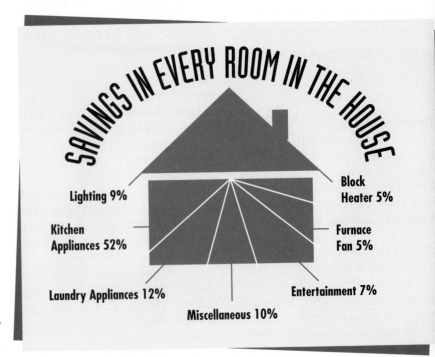

SAVINGS IN EVERY ROOM IN THE HOUSE

Lighting 9%

Kitchen Appliances 52%

Laundry Appliances 12%

Miscellaneous 10%

Block Heater 5%

Furnace Fan 5%

Entertainment 7%

How Not to Buy a Lemon

So, you want a car. A new one is out of your price range, so you're looking into getting a "previously loved" vehicle. To avoid ending up with something that no-one in their right mind could possibly ever want, there are a few guidelines to follow.

1. Decide what you want

Before you even start looking for a car, decide how much you can afford to spend - not just on the purchase price of the car, but also on insurance, gas, licensing, etc. You should also draw up a list of the things your car has to do for you: Are you planning to drive in snowstorms? Will you be doing much highway driving? How many people will you be transporting, and what kind of cargo? When you've decided on a price range for your car, and your list of needs, it's time to start looking around.

2. Do your research

The newspapers are full of ads for cars for sale, and there are many publications advertising only used vehicles. You can also wander around a couple of used car lots (but be prepared to fend off the salespeople!), and check out cars with "For Sale" signs taped to their windows. All this sniffing around should give you a good idea of what kind of car you can get for your money, and might even turn up a vehicle you're interested in buying.

You'll probably notice that vehicles being sold privately tend to be less expensive than those for sale through a used car dealer. There are two reasons for this: the dealer has to make money to cover the overheads; and the dealer may be including some kind of warranty.

If you don't see something you really like, keep on looking. Don't settle for "OK" when tomorrow you might find "Perfect!"

3. Check it out

Once you've located a vehicle that looks like it fits the bill, it's time to get really serious about checking it out. This can be done in three stages: a curbside check, a test-drive, and a professional mechanic's diagnostic.

The curbside check is something you can do yourself, but there are so many things to look for, it'll make your head spin, so make a list ahead of time. Include things like tires, rust spots, seatbelts, lights (all of them), brakes, radio, windows, door catches and locks, windshield wipers, paint job. It's almost essential to take a friend with you (the more knowledgeable, the better) to turn things on while you check them, and note down your comments. And, of course, you'll be able to see best if you go during daylight hours.

If you are pretty satisfied with the results of your curbside check, it's time for a test drive. Drive the car yourself, and pay attention to what you're doing. Ask your friend to make a note of any unusual quirks you notice, like difficulty shifting gears, odd noises, sloppy brakes, exhaust smoke. If possible, include some highway driving and some street driving, and go to a place (such as an empty lot) where you can stop and start, reverse, drive without holding the steering wheel, and turn tight circles.

After a satisfactory test drive, ask to see all the vehicle's paperwork. Was the previous owner a taxi-cab company? Are there any liens against the car (i.e. is it in danger of being repossessed because the previous owner didn't pay all the lease payments)? These sorts of things can be serious warning signs.

If you're happy with everything you've seen so far, it's time to arrange for a professional to check out the vehicle. If the person selling the car doesn't go for this, then walk away. If there's anything to hide, you want to know about it before you buy the car, right?

4. Get a mechanic's opinion

Mechanics should be prepared to spend an hour or so looking at your potential purchase, but you should be prepared to pay for this expertise. Allow about $100. The mechanic will check out the engine, the frame, and all the other bits that they're paid to understand and you're not. If your curbside check and test drive turned up any problems, mention these to the mechanic, too, and ask for a written estimate of how much it would cost to do any essential or recommended repairs. Do you still want to buy this vehicle?

5. Agree on a price

Armed with your mechanics report and estimate, it's time to haggle. Stick to your guns. It's your budget, remember, and you've got to live with it if you pay more than you can afford. On the other hand, don't lose a good vehicle by being too cheap. You may be asked to put your offer in writing. This is your last chance to back out, because once a written offer is accepted, you've bought the car.

6. Buy it!

You'll probably have to pay by certified cheque - that way the seller is certain of getting his money. In exchange, make sure you get a bill of sale for the vehicle, plus the ownership papers and copies of any warranties, etc. you and the seller have agreed on.

Don't drive your new baby home unless you are insured to do so! You will also need to have the car registered in your name, and it will need licence plates (look in the Blue Pages for the nearest Vehicle Registration office).

Car Collision Musts

1. STOP - no matter how minor the accident.
2. Care for the injured, and send for help and for the police.
3. Remove any hazards from the road.
4. Warn oncoming traffic.
5. Get information: write down the condition of the road, the weather. Get the name, address, and telephone numbers of the other driver, anyone who is injured, witnesses. Also, record all the insurance information from the other driver and give your insurance information.
6. Record only the facts of the accident, not opinions.
7. Make no statements - sign no statements (except to police officers).
8. Safeguard your valuables - your purse or wallet. Lock them in your car if possible.
9. Notify your insurance agents or company.

Walking Down the Aisles

- Grocery Shopping 101

Assuming that you are buying for one or two people, and do not have access to a huge discount warehouse, you'll probably be following the usual routine of a weekly visit to a large grocery store or supermarket. Here you'll pick up most of what you'll need for the week. For advice on grocery shopping without breaking the bank, read on!

★ Try to get everything you need to last you the week, because it's frustrating to discover, two days later, that you've run out of ketchup or bathroom tissue. It's also expensive to buy these items from the convenience store on the corner (where most things do cost more), so avoid shopping there unless it's an emergency.

★ Make up a shopping list before you set out. Think of the following categories: house cleaning stuff; personal/bathroom stuff; breakfast food; lunch food; dinner food (make sure you include choices from all the food groups); condiments (ketchup, salt, herbs and spices); drinks. Or mentally walk around the grocery store, thinking of all the things on the shelves: which do you need? Some people keep a shopping list on the fridge, adding things as they think of them or as their supply starts to run low.

★ Don't go shopping when you're hungry: you'll probably end up buying about four different things that you could have for dinner when you get home. Or four things you could have for dessert. Eat first, shop after.

★ If you look closely the next time you go to a grocery store, you will notice that the bare necessities - bread, cheese, milk, fruit and veg., etc. - tend to be around the perimeter of the store. So, if you are really short of money, stick to this circuit, pick up the basics, and don't even venture up and down the aisles, where temptation lurks.

★ If or when you do venture along the aisles, your eyes will be assaulted by attractive packaging, "sale" stickers, coupons, and anything else the marketing experts can dream up to get you to buy their product. Lower your eyes, and check out the bottom shelf. This is where you'll find the cheaper brands, or the house brand. Often costing 30% less than the well-known brands (because they don't spend money on advertising) and just as good for taste and nutrient value, they are generally by far the best buy. You'll also find that buying things in larger packages is generally (but not always) cheaper. Look carefully at the price tags. Do a bit of mental math and calculate how much you are paying per 100g of food, or per item. Some stores have already calculated this for you, and display the information on the shelf price tag. To really take advantage of buying in bulk, you could form a co-op with a group of like-minded friends: buy big packages, and split them between you.

David De Lossy/Image Bank

is: learn to cook! It will save you a great deal of money, and will probably result in you eating more healthy foods. You see, food processing companies add a lot of salt, fat, preservatives and other additives to their products. If you use fresh ingredients, eat your creations promptly and store your left-overs in the fridge or freezer, you won't need these chemicals in your food.

★ Try not to give in to impulses if you can't afford them. The canned lobster would make Saturday night's pasta really special, but do you really have a spare $16?

★ If you are on a really tight budget, and cannot afford to go even a dollar over, you could invest in a cheap calculator and add up the cost of your purchases as you toss them in your cart. If you go over your limit, decide what is the least important item, and return it to the shelves. Bear in mind, though, that some items carry tax, which will be added on at the cash desk. If you are not sure what is taxable, the general rule is that grocery items, that you would prepare and serve at home (e.g. six bagels) are exempt from GST, while something that might be eaten as a snack (e.g., one bagel) will have GST added on. Of course, every province has its own rules for Provincial Sales Tax.

★ Finally, supplying your own grocery bags can save you a few cents at the checkout desk.

★ Some supermarkets have "sale racks" of bakery goods that are nearing their sell-by date. If you are going to eat them within a day or two, or if you can throw them straight into the freezer, these can be a great buy. A word of warning, though: soft baked goodies, such as dinner rolls and croissants, do not improve with age! Stale rolls with dinner aren't great, whereas sliced bread can be toasted and is

none the worse for being a day past its best. Don't pick up more than you can use, though: tossing a furry green loaf in the garbage is still a waste, even if you did get two for a dollar!

★ You may be lucky enough to have a really good fruit market, cheese store or delicatessen near your home. If you do, check the prices there and compare them with those at the supermarket. If they are the same or less, you can really take advantage of them, and pick up fresh cheese, meat or fruit whenever you need it. However, if the local stores are more expensive, restrain yourself from using them unless they have something you just can't get elsewhere.

★ Generally, the more highly-processed the food is, the more expensive it is. Pre-packaged fish and chips costs more than the raw fish and potatoes would, just as an oven-ready lasagna costs more than the basic ingredients to make it. The obvious conclusion, therefore,

FAQ Employment Insurance

♦ Employment Insurance (EI) provides Canadians with basic income protection. EI is like any other form of insurance: you must contribute a certain amount (a premium) into the plan before you can qualify for payments from the plan.

♦ Every paid hour you work will count toward qualification for EI. A minimum of 420 to 700 hours are required, depending on the unemployment rate in your region. If you are filing a claim after your first job, or after an absence of two years or more from the work-

force, you need 910 hours to qualify. To qualify for sickness, maternity or parental benefits, a minimum of 600 hours is required.

♦ The number of weeks payable to you is 14 to 45, depending on the hours of insurable employment and the rate of unemployment in your area.

♦ Like any other insurance plan, there are penalties for fraud, including more hours needed to qualify and fines.

New Roommate?

Don Eastcott wasn't your typical 20-year-old when he pulled up stakes from his family home in Rossland, B.C.

He had bucks and an entrepreneurial personality that saw him running his own construction company for seven years. And he could cook.

But his money and go-for-the-gold wisdom didn't save the future chief of the Canadian Organization of Small Business from the culture shock faced by most young people when they face their first apartment in a strange place.

"I wanted to get out. It was too confining. The rules of the house were too confining."

There were a lot of other rules to be learned, however.

> ## "You have to learn to think for yourself."

"You have to learn to think for yourself. It was a matter of learning to budget your time. No one told me how much time it takes to take care of your own mess — the laundry, the dishes, washing the floors."

Shopping for food could be a major expedition. "I think I packed a lunch.

"And it was a lot easier to cook at mom's house where everything was in place."

About two months into glorious independence, Eastcott ran into an unexpected problem.

"The loneliness was killing me."

Enter Keith, roommate *extraordinaire*, cooker of canned spaghetti over toast.

"It was a big mistake."

Eastcott said he came fully trained in the arcane arts of cooking, sewing and general housekeeping — it has been bred into his personality.

Keith was as untrained as an unhousebroken pup and "I wound up taking care of him. The only thing he could cook was canned spaghetti over toast." He bought cases of the stuff.

Keith did him a big favor, though; he taught Eastcott the importance of asking a lot of questions of prospective roomies and laying down firm ground rules about sharing the work and expenses of communal living.

"I'd be very critical. I'd put him through the third degree."

Eastcott's own three kids were all out by the time they were 20, under a flexible "18 and fly" rule in his household.

Menu

Monday: Spaghetti on toast

Tuesday: Spaghetti on toast

Wednesday: Spaghetti on toast

Thursday: Spaghetti on toast

Friday: Spaghetti on toast

Ask Questions

"We made sure they knew what they had to do. How to take care of themselves and allocate their time and money."

Moving out is all part of growing up and he says he's dismayed at statistics showing kids are staying home longer — or coming back if times get tough.

Maybe expectations are too high — they don't want to leave because they have it too good where they are.

They enjoy all the gadgets their parents have hanging around for their enjoyment — from color televisions, to real beds, convenient laundry facilities, microwaves, VCRs and transportation.

"A lot of them want the whole bloody works. They've never had to work to accumulate things."

Making do is all part of the process in the lean starting-out years, he said. "What did it take to make a coffee table? Twelve empty boxes, I think."

Sleeping on the floor in a sleeping bag and foamy is the ideal first bed. Kraft dinner and Ichiban noodles won't kill anyone — at least in the short term.

What's the priority? What do you do until the television comes? He has no problem with a kid making a stereo a priority. "Music is important — music and books."

> *"...No one told me how much time it takes to take care of your own mess — the laundry, the dishes, washing the floors."*

Reprinted with permission of UNITED FEATURE SYNDICATE.

How to
choose, keep, or lose
a roommate

A roommate is someone who is going to see you at your very worst: when your hair is unwashed first thing in the morning; when you have a cold and your nose is red and peeling; when you've run out of clean clothes, and you have to wear something from your bedroom floor. Nothing is hidden from roommates. You share a kitchen, a bathroom, perhaps even a bedroom. Think carefully about who you want to know this much about you. And think just as carefully about who you want to know this much about. Can you handle having underwear dripping in the bathtub every day? How do you feel about someone finishing the milk, and not replacing it? Is it important to you that you always get to sit in the right-hand corner of the couch?

Choosing

Before you let a roommate into your life, think about the things that are important to you. It might be that you don't mind taking on one chore, providing the roommate takes responsibility for an equivalent job. Perhaps one of you could keep the kitchen clean and the other one handle the bathroom, or one do the grocery shopping and the other the vacuuming and floor-washing. But if you believe that the only fair way is to split every chore right down the middle, you'll want someone who's idea of a clean bathroom is not too far from yours. In other words, you need to consider just exactly what you expect of your new roomie. Why not write a list, adding things as you think of them? The list can be used to generate discussion with a potential roomie.

Finding a roommate is a bit like finding your life partner - it may be the kid you played with in grade school, or you may have to travel across the country before you find the perfect person. And it's just as important to ask lots of questions. If possible, see them in their natural habitat, too. If they're presently living in a spotless, tidy, well-regulated place, chances are they're not going to fit in with your freewheeling, casual, do-it-when-you-have-to lifestyle, or vice versa.

When interviewing potential candidates, consider your requirements, and those of the other person. As well as similar standards of cleanliness, it is important that you both agree on smoking policy, friends staying over, long-distance phone charges, etc. What's probably less important is that you have different styles of clothing or preferences in food. If you both don't mind cooking for yourselves every evening then it won't matter if your roommate doesn't know bannock from banana bread. However, for the serious issues, it might be a good idea to draw up a written contract, signed by the two of you, that will set the standards that you will both be expected to live up to.

Keeping

Once you have a roommate, you are bound to find that they do something to drive you crazy every single day. This is where your people skills come into play. Pick your battles. For each issue you have three options: letting it ride and just living with it; trying to tactfully address the issue, and possibly compromising on the outcome; or blowing your top and threatening to throw the offender out or to move out yourself. Each response is appropriate in certain situations, but make sure you don't get the wrong response for the wrong situation. For example, if your roomie loads the toilet paper on the holder so it hangs down

against the wall, instead of away from the wall, it might be appropriate to ignore this slight character flaw. But if the jerk steals all your money from your wallet during the night, you might be entitled to politely ask him or her to leave. For good.

Losing

So, how do you get rid of a roommate when it's not working out? It might be quite easy. If the person is a reasonable human being, he or she will realize that the two of you are just not meant to be. Nine times out of ten, the other person will be just as unhappy with the arrangement as you are. After all, would you choose to stay in a situation where you felt as though you didn't fit in?

But occasionally you might find yourself stuck with a roommate who just won't take the subtle, or not so subtle, hints that you are giving about it being time to leave. If your roommate refuses to move out when asked point blank, what can you do about it? Well, there are not really a lot of options. Remember that, if you are the leaseholder (the person who signed the landlord's lease in the first place), you are responsible for any damage to the place, for ensuring that the landlord gets the rent owing, and for paying the utilities and other costs. If your roommate leaves under a cloud of bad feeling and refuses to pay his/her share of that month's rent etc., there's not really anything you can do about it. You will have to absorb the extra costs yourself. Similarly, if you are the leaseholder and you want to leave, you'll still have to give your landlord notice, or forfeit rent for the notice period. Even if you have a contract with your roommate, so you had officially sublet the space, you cannot generally evict a person without 90 days notice.

You'd probably be right to conclude that it would be better to make the parting of the ways as civil and as fair as possible, with each person helping to ease the transition. Could you offer to help the person find another place to live (although you may not feel like helping them, or even talking to them...), or could you suggest someone who might take your place if you are looking for another home for yourself?

Sharing your home is never easy, but it saves money, provides company, reduces the chores, and gives a feeling of security. To retain the good aspects, and reduce the not-so-good ones, make sure you state your expectations clearly at the beginning, keep the lines of communication open, and respect each others' feelings and dignity.

10 Tips *for living on your own*

1. Write down frequently-used and emergency phone numbers on a piece of card and pin it up near the phone.

2. Keep a running shopping list, adding items as you think of them.

3. If you hate housework, assign it to certain days of the week (e.g., Monday - clean kitchen; Tuesday - do laundry; etc.)

4. When (if!) you cook a meal, make more than you need so that you have enough for lunch the next day.

5. Have a safe place to put bills and other important mail as it arrives, if you can't deal with it right away, so it won't get lost or forgotten.

6. Pay off credit card bills right away - why pay for the privilege of worrying about them?

7. Any payments that have to be made regularly every month can be handled by the bank - automatic withdrawal (e.g., car insurance, dental insurance).

8. If you live alone and are tired of cooking for yourself and eating by yourself every day, arrange to alternate one meal a week with a friend: this week he cooks for you both; next week it's your turn. This works well for single-parent families, too, and is fun for the children.

9. Make sure that everyone in the house knows, and agrees on, where everything should be put away. There's nothing more frustrating than searching the house for the can-opener after your roommate has "cleaned up"!

10. If you're always in a rush to get out the door in the mornings, try setting everything ready the night before: clothes, shoes, lunch, even the cereal bowl on the table. Anything to cut down on stuff to do in the morning.

Low-Impact LIVING

by Margaret Atwood

During the 1930s and 40s - the depression and the war - conservation was a way of life. It wasn't called that. It was called saving, or salvaging, or rationing. People saved things and reused them because raw materials were expensive or scarce. They saved string, rubber bands, bacon fat, newspapers, tin cans and glass bottles, old clothes. They made new things out of old things; they darned socks, turned shirt collars. They grew Victory Gardens. "Waste not, want not" was their motto.

Then came the end of the war, a new affluence, and the Disposable Society. We were encouraged to spend and waste; it was supposed to be good for the economy. Throwing things out became a luxury. We indulged.

We can no longer afford our wasteful habits. It's Back to the Basics, time for a return to the Three Rs: *Reduce. Reuse. Recycle. Refuse*, too, to buy polluting products, and *rethink* your behaviour. For instance, use less energy: cut your overhead and increase your profits, and stave off a tax hike. Dry your clothes on a rack: humidify your home and lower your hydro bill. Leave excess packaging at the store: let them dispose of it. Manufacturers will get the message pretty quick, not just from you but from disgruntled retailers. Start a compost heap. Vote for politicians with the best environmental platforms.

Boden/Ledingham/Masterfile

Choose non-disposables: razors with real blades instead of the plastic chuck-it-out kind, fountain pens rather than toss-outs. Shop for organic veggies; do it using a shopping basket so you won't have to cart home all those annoying plastic bags that pile up under the sink. Lobby for country-of-origin labels on all food, so you know you aren't eating destroyed Amazon rainforest with every hamburger bite.

Pollution control, like charity, must begin at home. It's true that industries are major polluters, but industries, in the final analysis, are market- and therefore consumer-driven. If enough of us refuse to buy polluting products, the manufacturers will go out of business. Even a small percentage swing in buying patterns can mean the difference between profit and loss.

This is wartime. Right now we're losing; but it's a war we can still win with some good luck, a lot of good will, and a great many intelligent choices. The choice is yours.

Does Buying Green Mean Paying More?

Not necessarily.

Some environmentally-friendly products cost more than their conventional counterparts; that's partly because retailers charge what the market will bear, and consumers have generally been willing to pay more for green items. Another factor is that manufacturers often need to make large capital investments to get a new product line going. But one of the key goals of being a Green Consumer is to reduce overall consumption, so Green Consumers could end up paying less simply because they buy less.

Sustainable Development

helping to meet the needs of our generation and those of the future

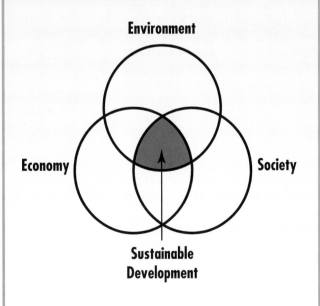

Environment

Economy

Society

Sustainable Development

COMPOUND IT

— and Know What You're Doing

The people who reallly win with their money are those who understand the power of compound interest. Compound interest is the money paid on the money and interest you made the year before. That's why the true power of compound interest takes a few years to show itself off in its best style. For example, if you invest $1 every year and leave it to compound, this is what happens:

Future Worth of One Dollar Invested at the End of Each Year with Interest Payable and Reinvested at the End of Each Year						
Year	1%	2%	3%	4%	5%	10%
1	1.00	1.00	1.00	1.00	1.00	1.00
2	2.01	2.02	2.03	2.04	2.05	2.10
3	3.03	3.06	3.09	3.12	3.15	3.31
4	4.06	4.12	4.18	4.25	4.31	4.64
5	5.10	5.20	5.31	5.42	5.53	6.10
10	10.46	10.95	11.46	12.01	12.58	15.94
20	22.02	24.30	26.87	29.78	33.07	57.27
30	34.78	40.57	47.58	56.08	66.44	164.49
40	48.89	60.40	75.40	95.03	120.80	442.59

Source: Deloitte & Touche,
Canadian Guide to Personal Financial Management, 11th Ed.

So if, at the end of every year for 40 years, you put a dollar into an account or investment that pays an interest rate of 5%, at the end of those 40 years you get an amazing $120.80 for your efforts. Yet, $120.80 for a dollar a year is not bad profit, considering you only invested $40. But who would bank one dollar a year for 40 years?.

The most important thing about this chart is the way you can really use it. Let's say you put away $8 a month - probably less than the cost of one movie. That's $96 a year. So at the end of the first year you will have $96. At the end of Year Two you have $192.96 ($96 X 2.01).

You get the multiplier amount from the chart that is based on a one dollar amount and the 1% interest rate.

Let's say that you cannot find anything better than 1% interest. Well, by Year 5, at one movie's worth a month, you'll have $519.60 ($96 X 5.10) -

not a bad sum of money for banking $8 a month for 5 years. You are not likely to miss the $8 each month. Just think of how much you spend a month - will $8 truly be missed?

But likely you will be able to find a savings account with better interest - let's say 2%. By putting away $10 a month, a total of $120 a year, you will have saved $120 at the end of the first year. By the end of Year Two, at 2%, you will have $242.40 (remember that the multiplier number takes into account the fact that you have contributed another $120 in the second year).

Do the same thing - bank $10 a month for 4 years at 2%, and the total for your efforts will be , and you will have $494.40, almost $500 savings without really missing any big

amount of money each month.

These are pretty short term amount. and investments. If you find a sav ings/investment account at 5% for : years, and put $10 a month in it, at the end of the term you will have $663.60 At ten years, you will have $1509.60

Try doing the figuring yourself Choose an amount you can bank eacl month. Find the best interest-bearing account you can. Then calculate wha your money will be earning for you You can even have the amount yo have chosen to save withdrawn di rectly from your chequing account and directly deposited into your saving: account each month. You can mak this arrangement with your bank.

How do you get better interes rates? One way is to have the smalle amounts that you have saved, let's say $500 or $1000, moved into a highe interest-bearing investment such as a GIC (Guaranteed Investment Certificate or Term Deposit. Usually you have t leave your money in such an invest ment for a longer period o time but the interes rate is higher and your money i working harder fo you.

One loony will:

- roast 2 turkeys in your oven
- run your microwave oven for 12 hours
- let you play video games for 34 days, 2 hours per day
- operate a 1,500-watt portable electric heater for 10 hours
- operate your frost-free (older model) fridge for two and a half days
- light 3 strings of outdoor mini-lights (25 lights per string) for 73 days, 4 hours per day
- light 3 strings of 5-watt outdoor Christmas lights (25 lights per string) for 10 days, 4 hours per day
- cook 5 batches of Boston Baked Beans in your slow cooker
- make 33 steaming loaves of bread in your breadmaker
- let you watch 57 movies on your VCR/TV
- make 50 freshly-brewed pots of coffee
- run your electric drill for 50 hours
- humidify the air for 6 days

Note: This may vary from province to province

Let the Good Times Roll:

a surge in teenage spending is helping to keep the economy in gear

by David Fischer and Michele Meyer

When 18-year-old Jon Angle set his sights on a $5,000 motorcycle last month, he was determined not to let a little thing like lack of funds stand in his way. "My bank said they'd never loan me that sort of money, since I don't really have any assets yet," the recent high school graduate from Littleton, Colo., recalls. Still, Angle was able to secure a loan from the Young Americans Bank in Denver, which caters to the under-22-year-old crowd and permits allowance to be listed as a source of income on loan applications. Now, with a new Suzuki, Angle is setting aside most of the income from his $6.75-an-hour job at a local McDonald's to pay off his debt.

At malls, movie theaters and even motorcycle dealerships around the country, teenagers like Jon Angle are behaving like the fiscal equivalent of the Energizer Bunny: They keep spending, and spending, and spending. Last year, 12-to-19-year-olds went on their biggest shopping spree ever, ringing up 109 billion in purchases, a 38 percent increase. And the demographics for the teen market are enough to make any orthodontist smile. As the baby boomers' babies hit puberty, the teen population is expected to balloon from 29.1 million to 34.9 million by 2010.

Teens also are earning money. About half of all 16-to-19-year-olds have part-time jobs, according to Teenage Research Unlimited, a market research firm. Combined with allowance from their parents, adolescents average $64 in income per week. But that money burns a quick hole in their pockets. For every dollar teens earned last year, they spent 84 cents. And even when they do put aside some of their funds, teenagers save only until they can afford some coveted big-ticket item. Claire Boetticher, 17, from North Dallas, Texas, for example, received $35 in weekly allowance and is earning an extra $100 a week this summer working on a ranch. She spends most of the money on food, movies and compact disks. And when Boetticher does save, she usually hangs onto the money only long enough to buy tickets to a rock concert.

With all this money up for grabs, it is no longer just makers of acne medication who are zeroing in on adolescents. Nike, for example, which consistently ranks as one of the most popular brands among teens, targets its products to consumers between the ages of 14 and 24. And Levi Strauss consults a panel of several hundred teens around the country during its product-development process. If the feedback indicates that the cut on a pair of jeans needs changing, the designers return to the drawing board.

Teens don't just spend their own money, they also affect the way their parents shop. When it comes time to buy a family computer, for instance, grown-ups often turn to their kids as technology consultants. With children using PCs at school, it's not surprising that parents who buy home computers let their teens influence the decision about two thirds of the time.

Shopping. As single-parent and dual-wage families become more prevalent today, adolescents also are playing a bigger role in the purchase of more mundane household goods. Even though they may wish to avoid such chores, 83 percent of all teens now do at least some of their family's grocery shopping. Food manufacturers have taken notice. "The packaging of supermarket products," observes Audrey Guskey of Dupuesne University, "is being made brighter to catch the eye of young shoppers."

Companies that target teenage consumers hope to develop long-term brand loyalty. General Motors publishes a magazine on safe driving that is distributed to over 13,000 high schools and drivers education programs each year. The stories feature safety tips and driving advice, but they also contain photos of GM cars and trucks. The auto giant isn't the only company trying to make sure its name is on the tip of teens (pierced or unpierced) tongues. Ads for everyday products like soup and laundry detergent, for example, have begun appearing on MTV. Choosing between powder and liquid detergent isn't very appealing to most teenagers, but companies know that if they can get teens to buy their products now, they have a good chance of keeping them as customers for years. Judging from the way this next generation is spending money, that seems to be an investment worth making.

It Came From Outer Scalp

To put a little gleam back in your hair, shampoo it less often so your natural oil can come shining through. Using a conditioner will also help smooth down those shingles and tame the electrical charge.

My friends call me the Crisco Kid. Do I need a special shampoo for my oily hair?

You have the opposite problem. Like many teens, you have overactive glands in your scalp. They're secreting too much oil, making your hair greasy. Every shampoo contains detergents to clean hair, as well as conditioning ingredients to keep hair from getting too clean and drying out.

Shampoos formulated for oily hair adjust the balance of cleansers and moisturizers to maximise grease removal and manageabilty. But which shampoo you use doesn't matter nearly as much as your scrubbing schedule. You just need to lather up more often — with *any* shampoo.

Help! How can I tame this dry hair?

For starters, put away that blow-dryer! What you're battling is a bad case of dull, flyaway hair, which can only get worse with blow-drying. In normal, healthy hair, oil secreted by the scalp smoothes down the "shingles" of each hair so they lie flat and shine. When the shingles stick up, they tangle with each other and don't reflect light well. Add in dry hair's static electricity, and you've got that flyaway look.

Mom says if I start perming my hair now, I'll look like Homer Simpson by the time I'm 20. Am I doomed to a life without curls?

Perms use chemicals to break down the bonds in your hair's cortex. The hair is then wrapped around rods, and other chemicals lock in the curls. A decade of perms won't turn you into Homer's bowling-ball twin. But it won't win you a spot in a long-glossy-hair shampoo commercial either. Perms weaken hair and dry it out. So do chemical straighteners for curly hair.

For temporary, chemical-free curls, try rolling up your damp hair in rags overnight: You'll have Shirley Temple corkscrews in the morning. Or let your hair dry in braids for a crimped, wavy look. To go from wavy to straight, blow-dry your hair, pulling it straight with a round brush. Then use a hair iron to press away any stubborn curls. But be warned: All that heat can make your hair dry and brittle, and can lead to split ends.

Ads say I should "nourish my hair." Do I feed it apple custard, fatty acids, or Pro-V vitamins? I've also heard eggs will make it shiny. Should I use sunny-side up or scrambled?

Advertisers may want you to believe your hair is screaming out for fatty acids, or needs an apple a day. But the truth is, hair is dead. It doesn't have much of an appetite, and you can't nourish it. You're better off feeding *yourself* a healthful diet with enough protein and vitamins to keep the body that produces that hair healthy.

But conditioners can *help* your hair — not by nourishing it, but by coating the hair shaft and smoothing down its shingles. As for eggs? Like conditioners, the protein in raw eggs can coat and smooth your hair. But cracking an egg over your head has major drawbacks: Handling raw eggs can bring you in contact with the dangerous salmonella virus. And if you don't rinse well, you could start smelling like last week's lunch.

My dandruff is so bad, I'm considering a mini-vac for my head. What else can I do?

Dandruff is just the normal shedding of your scalp's dead skin cells. Shampooing usually gets rid of the flakes, but oily scalps (not dry, as many believe) can produce larger flakes that are more difficult to wash away. If your favorite blue sweater looks like a ski slope, try a specially-formulated dandruff shampoo, which can keep dead skin cells from clumping together in big flakes.

My hair won't stay fluffed when I blow it dry. Do I have to take it to obedience school to get it to do what I want?

Just glue it — with styling gel or mousse. Those products cling to the hair shaft, then dry, holding whatever do you've created. By coating the hair shaft, they also make it thicker, adding body to hair. Unfortunately, sticky sprays and gooey gunk also attract dirt, dust, and dead skin cells. It's hard to shine under all that build-up. You'll have to haul out the shampoo more often.

I'm ready to embrace my inner redhead. Will coloring my hair damage it?

That depends on the kind of dye you use. Hair gets its color from pigment in the cortex of the hair shaft. Altering your hair's color permanently — lighter or darker — requires harsh chemicals to penetrate the hair shaft. The process causes hair to lose some of its natural protection and ability to hold moisture, so color-processed hair tends to dry out easily.

Semi-permanent dyes wash out after a few shampoos and don't break down the cortex. They chemically color the outside of the hair shaft, and so are a bit gentler on the hair.

Henna, made from the dried leaves of the Lawsonia plant, permanently colors the outside of the hair shaft. It's natural, but not perfect. It's hard to predict what color you'll get. And henna seals the shaft completely, locking moisture out, and leaving you dry.

Before Grecian formula, ancient Egyptians covered their gray hair with an ointment made of one part paw of dog, one part kernel of date, and one part hoof of donkey.

In the 16th and 17th century in England, tennis balls were stuffed with human hair to give them bounce.

People in commercials always have perfect hair. Ads make shampoos and conditioners seem like magic love potions. I've tried a million brands, and I still have no one to kiss but my dog.

Of course ads show perfect people with flawless hair! They're selling an image, so you'll buy the product. If you had a personal stylist hovering over your head of hair, you'd look like a TV commercial, too.

As tests over the years have shown, all shampoos and conditioners are basically created equal. The biggest difference is not how they clean or condition your hair, but how they smell. No shampoo can guarantee you dates. But with the mind-boggling selection out there, you're sure to find a scent that Rover likes!

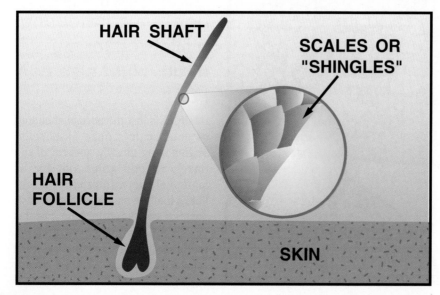

HAIR SHAFT

SCALES OR "SHINGLES"

HAIR FOLLICLE

SKIN

What Does It Say On The Label?

A food label can give you a lot of information. Here's the "who" and "what" of label-reading.

Agriculture Canada is responsible for inspection and grading of foods such as meat, eggs, canned or frozen foods. The grade tells you the food is safe and what to expect about appearance or size. For instance, Canada Choice canned foods will probably be more uniform in size and shape than Canada Standard. Utility Grade poultry may have a tear in the skin or perhaps a wing missing. Grades do not affect the nutritive quality. Imported foods must meet Canadian standards and are inspected by Agriculture Canada at the borders.

Health Canada regulates what claims can be made for foods. For instance, it is illegal to say that a food will prevent or cure diseases. You can say that a nutrient is "a factor in maintaining good health." The manufacturer is not required to give you nutrition information, but if he chooses to, he must follow guidelines. For example, if he says his food is low in fat, he must meet the federal guideline of three grams of fat or less per serving. Then he has to tell you what a serving is and he has to print the analysis of the food. If he

wants to tell you that his food contains a certain vitamin or mineral then a serving must provide a minimum of 5% of your total daily requirement. He can say his food is "a source" or "a good source" or "high" depending on how much of the nutrient is present. Again, he has to back up his claim by printing the nutrient analysis. Consumer and Corporate Affairs Canada is responsible for enforcing all of these standards. In addition, they require that a food package include:

- the common name of the food
- the weight or volume in the package
- the ingredients in descending order of proportion
- the name and address of the company.

Foods with a shelf life of 90 days or less must have a "best before" date — except fresh meat, which has to indicate the date it was packaged. Most foods are still safe after that date, but flavour or texture may be affected.

The ingredient list can give you a pretty good idea about the nutritional value of the food. If the first few ingredients are fats or sugars, you can be fairly sure that the food isn't going

to be the best choice from a nutrition point of view. If the first three or four ingredients listed are foods that would fit into a food group, you're probably making a good choice.

If you're buying a food because of its nutrition claims, read the label carefully. The nutrition information box will tell you what's present in a serving, but unless you know what your daily requirement is, what good is the information? Look for the percentage of your daily requirement offered in a serving of the food.

Be aware that some information is misleading even though it's true. For instance, some food products are labelled "cholesterol free." If the fat in that food is a vegetable oil, it's true that it won't have cholesterol, but it could still be very high in fat. The best way to control your blood cholesterol is to reduce total fat intake, and that particular food might not be a good choice for you.

Some food products make misleading statements on the label, such as implying that you need the product as a supplement, or that it will prevent illness. The package may not provide an ingredient list, or the name of the manufacturer. You'll have nowhere to start if you have an allergic reaction or any questions about the product.

Spotting Health Fraud

People waste billions annually on bogus treatments that promise to be simple solutions to better health.

To recognize a worthless treatment, ask:

Does it promise too much too easily?
— Unproven remedies are often promoted as cure-alls, from preventing aging to curing impotence.

Does it claim immediate or guaranteed results?
— Few medical treatments produce immediate benefits for chronic conditions. And even proven therapies can't always guarantee better health.

Does it include a secret or exclusive formula?
— Legitimate therapies evolve from data collected and reviewed by many scientists.

Are testimonials the only proof it works?
— Unproven remedies are typically endorsed by "satisfied customers." These people may be paid for their comments or lulled by the power of suggestion into the belief they were "cured."

Does it offer a money-back guarantee?
— A guarantee is an effective ploy to get you to buy a product. But don't expect anyone to respond to your refund request.

How to Read the Stock

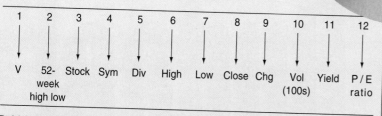

1	2	3	4	5	6	7	8	9	10	11	12
V	52-week high low	Stock	Sym	Div	High	Low	Close	Chg	Vol (100s)	Yield	P/E ratio

Bold-faced stocks closed yesterday at least 5 per cent higher or lower in price than the previous close. Stocks must close at a minimum $1.

Underlined stocks traded yesterday 500 per cent or more above their 13-week average daily volume (on Canadian exchanges only).

1. (Arrow up or down) — New 52-week high or low in day's trading.

2. 52-week high/low — Highest and lowest intra-day price in past 52 weeks.

3. Stock — Abbreviated company name.

4. Sym — Ticker symbol assigned to issue by exchange; .PR is preferred share, .WT is warrant, .UN is unit, .S means stocks are subject to regulation of the SEC Act, W means when issued.

5. Div — Indicated annual dividend (excluding special dividends).

6. High — Highest intra-day trading price.

7. Low — Lowest intra-day trading price.

8. Close — Closing price.

9. Chg — Change between closing price and previous closing board lot price.

10. Vol — Number of shares traded in 100s; z preceding figure indicated sales are reported in full.

11. Yield — Expressed as percentage, calculated by dividing the dividend by current market price.

12. P/E ratio — Price/earnings ratio; current stock price divided by the company's earnings per share from continuing operations for the latest 12 months. The P/E ratio is not shown if greater than 100.

Footnotes

a — in U.S. dollars (for Canadian exchanges)

au — in Australian dollars

b — in British pounds or pence

c — in Canadian dollars (on U.S. exchanges)

ci — commercial/industrial stock (on the Vancouver Stock Exchange)

da — dividend in arrears

dc — dividend paid in Canadian dollars, but stock trades in U.S. dollars

g — coming capital gains distribution will be paid to the current owner

in — inactive stock (on the VSE)

j — subject to special reporting rules

n — stock is new issue

ni — mutual fund with no front-end load or contingent deferred sales load

nv — non-voting

rc — in bankruptcy or receivership or being reorganized under the Bankruptcy Act, or securities assumed by such companies

rf — redemption fee or contingent deferred sales load may apply

rs — resources stock (VSE)

rv — shareholders' voting is restricted

s — indicates 52-week high-low range has been adjusted to reflect stock split or consolidation

sv — subordinate-voting

x — stock is trading ex-dividend

Data supplied by Dow Jones Telerate Canada Inc. To comment or make suggestions about our stock or commodity quotations, please call 416-585-5500. You can also reach us on the Internet at stocks@GlobeAndMail.ca

FREE Annual Reports Service

This is a free reader service. You can obtain the annual reports and, if available, quarterly reports, of any companies for which the ♣ symbol appears. To order, please call 1-800-965-6199 or give stock symbols of the companies whose reports you want and fax your request to 1-800-617-678. Open 24 hours, including weekends. Reports will be sent the next working day, subject to availability, by first class mail.

52-week high	low	Stock	Sym	Div	High	Low	Close	Chg	Vol (100s)	Yield	P/E ratio
					A—B						
50	1.05	ABL Cda	ABL		1.25	1.18	1.18	+0.02	76		
.60	3.80	♣ ACC Tele	ACL		21.50	21.50	21.50	+0.25	1		24.7
/2	3.00	AFM Hospit	AFM		3.10	3.10	3.10		5		
50	17 1/4	AGF Ma	AGF.B	0.60	32.25	31.90	32.25	+0.05	143	1.9	23.9
.05	10.00	♣ AGRA	AGR	0.16	11.00	10.60	10.60	-0.15	28	1.5	15.6
5/8	3.5	AIT Advanc	AIV		4.40	4.10	4.10	-0.20	115		
6	.035	AJ Perron	AJP		0.07	.065	.065	-.005	288		
0	0.27	AQM Auto	AQV		0.31	0.30	0.30	+0.01	200		
5	0.80	ARC Resin	ASR		0.85	0.80	0.80	-0.11	10		
85	11 1/2	♣ AT Plasti	ATP	0.18	13.80	13.70	13.80	+0.05	578	1.3	10.6
90	8 1/2	♣ ATt Techs	ATY		15.65	15.50	15.60	-0.05	266		26.9
00	19 1/2	ATS Autom	ATA		43.75	42.50	43.50	-0.40	58		30.4
50	2.95	♣ Abacan	ABC		12.00	11.60	11.70	-0.20	955		
85	8	Aber j	ABZ		19.50	19.30	19.45	-0.05	733		
/2	16.50	Abi	A		20	19.95	20.20	+0.05	3113	2.0	8.6
	0.42	A	CU						1158		
									2636		
									166		

52-week low	high	Stock	Sym	Div	High	Low	Close	Chg	Vol (100s)	Yield	P/E ratio
16.15	12.55	♣ Acetex	ATX		13.25	12.55	12.55	-0.60	14		13.5
18.00	9 1/4	Acklands	ACK		17.10	17.00	17.10	+0.10	58		16.8
1.70	0.60	Adex Mira	AMG	0.11	0.64	0.60	0.61	-0.01	734	17.5	
7 1/2	3.20	♣ Adrian Rs	ADL		4.00	3.45	3.75		272		
0.95	0.50	Advancd M	AMR		0.72	0.70	0.70	-0.01	440		10.4
0.84	0.27	Advantex	ADX		0.40	0.40	0.40		473		
4.40	1.40	Advntre	AVN		1.45	1.45	1.45	+0.05	z27		
29.25	26 1/2	Bk NS	BNS.PR.F		1.78	29.25	29.15	29.15		20	6.1
29.25	26	Bk NS	BNS.PR.G		1.75	29.10	29.10	29.10	+0.10	5	6.0
29.00	25 1/4	Bk NS	BNS.PR.H		1.69	28.65	28.50	28.65	+0.15	33	5.9
11.75	9 1/4	Brk NS	BNS.UN		0.67	11.60	11.50	11.50		220	5.8
x45	33.50	Barrick Gld	ABX	a0.14	40.25	39.00	39.65	+0.65	71221	0.5	36.5
6.45	3.15	♣ Barringt j	BPL		6.25	6.10	6.15		3209		41.0
12	8.20	Baton	BNB		8.50	8.40	8.40	-0.10	7		
3.60	0.85	Battery Tech	BTI		1.19	1.11	1.11	-0.09	350		
1		Battle Mtn	BMC		10.00		10.00	+0.25	4455		
			BTE					-0.20	951		

Building a Budget

A budget is a working document. You write your own budget and then you use it, on a regular basis, for your own benefit, your own financial management. In a budget you keep track of the amount of money coming in and the amount of money going out. With any luck they will be the same, with perhaps a little left over for increased saving. Not in your case? Well, the amount coming in might be somewhat out of your control, but you can do something about the amount going out. First you have to know where it is going. And that's the value of a working budget.

The list in this article will give you some ideas about what you might write into your own working budget. Once you have set up your budget sheet, you can really get to work.

You use a working budget by

- ◆ regularly recording your expenses to track what you spend

- ◆ reviewing your budget every so often to see if you are on target with your plans

- ◆ making changes - additions and deletions - as they more accurately reflect your true spending habits

- ◆ paying attention to your budget so that it can guide you in your plans and choices about using money. A budget that is ignored is of no use at all.

Since money is just one of the resources you have, a budget is just one way you work towards the goals and lifestyle choices you have made.

Income

- part-time or full-time salary
- contract work
- bonuses, commissions
- interest income (from savings accounts, bonds, other investments)
- scholarships, bursaries
- other income (family support)

Expenses

(Divide annual expenses by 12 to calculate your monthly expenses)

- contribution to emergency fund
- contribution to savings account (paying yourself first)
- rent (or mortgage payment, condo fee)
- utilities (if averaged on a monthly plan)
  - gas
  - electricity
  - heat
  - phone rental and local calls
- insurance (if averaged on a monthly plan)
  - tenant
  - car
  - medical
  - disability
- day-care services
- recreation/ association dues (if averaged on a monthly plan)
- cable TV
- loan payments (car, computer, stereo, etc.)
- credit card payments (if your credit cards are not clear)

- taxes (if averaged on a monthly plan), including property taxes
- tuition fees
  - books, school supplies
- personal income tax
- other taxes (if not included in rent or mortgage)
- utilities (if not on an averaged plan)
  - electricity
  - heat
- insurance premiums (if not on a monthly plan)
  - tenant
  - car
  - disability
  - medical
- car registration
- driver's license fees
- car maintenance/repairs
- home maintenance/repairs
- transportation
  - bus tokens, passes, subway, taxis, etc.
  - gasoline/oil for car
  - parking
  - bicycle maintenance/repairs
- food
  - groceries including cleaning supplies, paper supplies
  - school and work lunches
  - other eating out
- clothing
  - smaller items
  - larger items (shoes, winter clothing, business suits - calculate costs and divide by 12)
  - laundry at public machines
  - laundry detergent/softener
  - dry-cleaning

- babysitting
- telephone
  - long distance
  - cellular
  - Internet connection
- furniture and household equipment
- health
  - medical
  - dental
  - over-the-counter drugs
  - prescriptions
  - birth control
- entertainment and recreation
  - community recreation facility fees (or club fees, sporting associations)
  - newspapers, magazines
  - books
  - video rentals
  - tobacco, alcohol
  - coffee out, movies, concerts, etc.
- pets
  - pet food
  - veterinary bills
- personal
  - personal items (shampoo, make-up, etc.)
  - haircuts, other hair treatments
  - charitable donations
  - major seasonal expenses (Christmas, Hanukkah) including gifts
  - other gifts
  - vacations
- other expenses and incidentals (postage, etc.)
- spending money

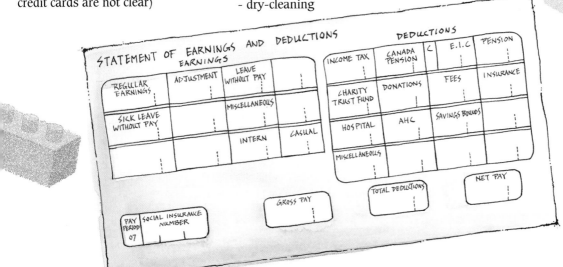

How the Government Sees It

If you spent $150 more than you earned last year, you got into a "deficit situation". You had a deficit of $150. How did you cover that? Borrowed from a buddy, the bank, or your Mom? However you did it, you ended up with a debt of $150. If, this year, you spend another $100 more than you earn, anybody can tell you that you now owe a total of $250. You have a deficit of $100 for the year (which is an improvement on last year), but you still have a total of $250 of debt.

Similarly, if a government borrows $150 million one year, and $100 million the next year, they say that their deficit has *decreased*. They borrowed *less* this year than last year!

FAQ   A Budget Fails Because...

♦ it is too complicated, covering pages and pages. A good budget fits on one page with general categories, which you really understand.

♦ you are confused about your categories in the budget. Write yourself a note explaining each of the general categories while you are first working on your budget.

♦ the budget isn't taken seriously. If you want a financial plan to work, you need to make your budget work.

♦ the budget is too tight. You need to give yourself some space, some breathing room, for little extras every once in a while.

♦ the estimations on what is spent are wrong. You need to be really honest with yourself about what you spend. For example, if you budget $12 for a movie but you also buy popcorn, a drink, and candy, then a night out at the movies is more likely to be $20.

♦ creating a budget is not a time for creating new limits for yourself; you need to begin with a realistic picture of your spending now.

♦ you are too negative about the process of budgeting. A budget is a tool to allow you to do what you really want with your money and not just let it slip out of your hands wondering where it all went. A budget can help you reach your goals.

♦ you don't keep track of what you spend. You need to have an accurate record of what you spend each month. You can choose to write down amounts as you spend them (a piece of paper in your wallet) or you can save every receipt and put them into an envelope at the end of the day. At the end of each month, sort the receipts into your categories and total them up. These records are important because they give you a real picture of your spending.

♦ its importance isn't recognized. The less income you have, the more important it is to have budget because there is less room for error.

♦ you've never tried it before you really need it. If you can, while you are still living at home, try to live on a budget you have calculated for yourself. Spend three months sticking to the limits for clothing, entertainment and other items.

TRUE CONFESSIONS of a COMPULSIVE BUDGETER

by Ron Chalmers

Budgets have an undeservedly bad rap, like diets—they deprive you of everything you want, they're no fun and they don't even work.

But Diane Davies says a budget helped her save—and was good, clean fun. Honest.

But she admits that she had all of the usual bad habits.

"I just never seemed to be able to save any money. I'd go to the bank my bank machine on Friday afternoon, take out this huge amount of money, and by Saturday noon I'm wondering: Where did I spend it all?"

To find the answer, she started carrying a note book in her purse, keeping track of everything she spent. Every penny.

Then she looked back at her spending record and asked herself: Are those really my priorities? Nope.

Would I have more fun using my money another way? Absolutely!

"I really do like budgeting," Davies discovered. "It really is fun."

And it's not like a diet: "Trust me, I'm a junk food addict and I find budgeting much easier than dieting."

The purpose of budgeting is simply "to put yourself in control of your money, making conscious decisions about how to make your money work for you," Davies says.

David Chilton writes in *The Wealthy Barber* that "budgeting doesn't work." Instead, he suggests saving 10 per cent of everything you earn "off the top." After that, let the spending take care of itself.

That may work for him but "I like a more structured process," Davies says. "And there are lots of other alternatives that might work better for you."

She follows four steps.

"First, determine how and what you spend now." You needn't track every penny, as Davies did, but "the more accurate, the better."

When people rely on memory, they lose track of 10 to 20 per cent of their spending.

"If carrying a notepad is too much work, you could save your receipts for a month, then tally them up," Davies suggests.

Reviewing her own spending habits was "a real shocker" she says:

"I would never have guessed that I spent that much on Christmas presents—or eating lunch out, every day."

Even afternoon trips to the drug store, for chocolate bars and other sugar fixes, were costing Davies more than $10 per week.

"Almost $600 a year—the price of an airplane ticket to Mexico!"

Her second step is to total the monthly income and all essential expenses.

"Third, set financial goals and priorities." This is decision time, when you compare your actual spending to your wish list—then decide what must go.

"Look at discretionary spending first," Davies says: "Things like eating out, and all those cable television channels."

The fourth step is to follow your program and monitor your progress.

"This is the really fun part," Davies says.

"Once you've identified your goals and set out a plan to achieve them, you'll be amazed at how motivated you'll be.

But do expect some social obstacles.

"Don't feel bad if your friends accuse you of being too cheap to go out to lunch regularly," Davies says.

"Just think how you'll feel when you're off on that dream vacation that they're only dreaming about—or when you're able to retire five years earlier because you were maximizing your RRSP when they were still struggling with credit card debts."

She offers a few tricks, so you won't bounce off the bandwagon:

"Don't try to achieve your financial goals overnight. A budget should not make you radically alter your lifestyle or really restrict your spending—or it becomes a chore, and you're not going to stick to it."

If you'll face occasional expenses such as insurance premiums or property tax, Davies suggest you save a regular amount each month. You also can budget a regular amount for big-ticket items—such as home renovations—that you've always wanted to buy, if only you had the "extra" money.

Remember that a budget is your tool—not your boss.

"Build in some room for flexibility and allow room for some mistakes," Davies says.

If you're especially accident prone, ask your employer to increase the income-tax withholding, as a forced savings plan.

You can arrange automatic bank transfers into a saving account.

And if you still spend too much, "give your credit card the cold shoulder by putting it in a bowl of water and freezing it for a while until you pay off your debts," Davies advises.

"Budgeting is easy—and anyone can do it!"

FAQ Net Worth

♦ If you have done any reading, you have probably come across the words "net worth". Simply, your net worth is all that you have of value minus all the you owe.

ASSETS - LIABILITIES = NET WORTH

♦ Net worth is important to know because it gives you a more global picture of how you are, financially. It may be that your financial worth right now *seems* to be very little but calculating your net worth once a year will tell you a lot about where, financially-speaking, you are going. For example, if your credit card debts have really increased but your cash and savings have not, you should realize that it's time to take action. Checking your net worth every so often helps you to be in control of your financial life.

♦ All that you own can include sports equipment, stereo equipment, any collectibles (such as coin or stamp collections), your car - you get the idea. You need to estimate the value of these items - what someone would pay you for them. Keep in mind that most things lose value as you own them, except perhaps for some collectibles. This is known as depreciation. Cars lose value with every year. In fact, new cars depreciate as soon as soon as they are driven off the lot. New cars depreciate by at least a third in the first year!

♦ Collectibles can also include antiques and art but relying on collectibles is riskier than most other forms of investing.

♦ All that you owe includes balances owed on credit cards, student loans, bank loans, and loans from friends and other people.

Tax Return

T1 GENERAL 1996

1

Revenue Canada / Revenu Canada

Individual Income Tax Return

Enter your social insurance number if it is not on the label, or if you are not attaching a label:

Step 1 – Identification

Attach your identification label here. Correct any wrong information.
If you are not attaching a label, print your name and address below.

First name and initial

Last name   Apt. or Unit No.

Address

City

Province or territory   Postal code

Enter your province or territory of residence on December 31, 1996:

If you were self-employed in 1996, enter the province or territory of self-employment:

If you became or ceased to be a resident of Canada **in 1996**, give the date of:

Day Month   or departure

entry   Day Month

	Day	Month	Year

Enter your date of birth:

Your language of correspondence: English ☐   Français ☐
Votre langue de correspondance :

If this return is for a deceased person, enter the date of death: Day Month Year   1 9

Check the box that applies to your marital status on December 31, 1996. We use it to determine the amount of certain credits and benefits.

1 ☐ Married   2 ☐ Living common-law   3 ☐ Widowed

4 ☐ Divorced   5 ☐ Separated   6 ☐ Single

If box 1 or 2 applies, enter your spouse's social insurance number if it is not on the label, or if you are not attaching a label:

Enter the first name of your spouse:

Check this box if your spouse was self-employed in 1996:   1 ☐

Do not use this area

Step 2 – Goods and services tax (GST) credit application
(You have to apply each year. See Step 2 in the guide to find out if you should apply this year.)

Are you applying for the goods and services tax credit? ....   Yes ☐ 1   No ☐ 2

If *yes*, enter the number of children under age 19 on December 31, 1996 (if applicable) ....

If *yes*, enter your spouse's net income from line 236 of your spouse's return (if applicable)

Step 3 – Total income

		101	
Employment income (box 14 on all T4 slips)	**102**	**104** +	
Commissions included on line 101 (box 42 on all T4 slips)		**113** +	
Other employment income (see line 104 in the guide)		**114** +	
Old Age Security pension (box 18 on the T4A(OAS) slip and box 24 on the T4A(P) slip)			
Canada or Quebec Pension Plan benefits (box 20 on the T4A(P) slip)	**152**	**115** +	
Disability benefits included on line 114 (see line 115 in the guide)		**119** +	
Other pensions or superannuation (see line 115 in the guide)		**120** +	
Employment Insurance benefits (box 14 on the T4U slip)		**121** +	
Taxable amount of dividends from taxable Canadian corporations (attach a completed Schedule 4)		**122** +	
Interest and other investment income (attach a completed Schedule 4)		Net **126** +	
Net partnership income: limited or non-active partners only (attach a completed Schedule 4)		**127** +	
Rental income	Gross **160**	Net **126** +	
Taxable capital gains (attach a completed Schedule 3)		**128** +	
Alimony or maintenance income		**129** +	
Registered retirement savings plan income (from all T4RSP slips)		**130** +	
Other income (see line 130 in the guide)	Specify:	Net **135** +	
Business income	Gross **162**	Net **137** +	
Professional income	Gross **164**	Net **139** +	
Commission income	Gross **166**	Net **141** +	
Farming income	Gross **168**	Net **143** +	
Fishing income	Gross **170**		
Workers' Compensation benefits (box 10 on the T5007 slip)	**144**		
Social assistance payments (see line 145 in the guide)	**145** +		
Net federal supplements (box 21 on the T4A(OAS) slip)	**146** +	▶ **147** +	
	Add lines 144, 145, and 146 =		
	Add lines 101, 104 to 143, and 147. This is your total income. **150** =		

600

Do not use this area	**605**				

5006-R

FAQ Insurance

- There is insurance for many things:

  Property, including your vehicle (truck, trailer, boat, motorized wheelchair), home (if you purchase home insurance), and the contents of your condo or apartment (if you get condominium/tenant insurance);

  Health (for medical treatments and, sometimes, for loss of wages), including out-of-country medical (medical treatments when you are out of Canada and need medical assistance);

  Travel/cancellation (if your tickets are not honoured or if you need to cancel your trip for specific serious reasons);

  Disability (if you become disabled and perhaps cannot work);

  Life insurance (which pays out to your dependants when you die).

- Personal insurance protects you from financial damages when something happens to you personally, including injury or death.

- Property insurance protects you, and sometimes others, from financial damage to property.

- Liability insurance protects you from being sued for property damage, or injury or death to other people.

- A policy is the written agreement between you and the insurance company.

- A premium is the amount you pay for the insurance.

- Coverage is the protection you get from the insurance you have purchased.

- A deductible is the amount you must pay on a claim before the insurance kicks in.

- Perils are the things that can happen that may be covered by your insurance and can include fire, lightning, theft, explosion, water damage, vandalism, windstorm, hail, glass breakage and many more incidents. However, it is very important to understand the policy before you buy because it will tell you specifically what is covered. Do not just assume that you have coverage for a bunch of perils.

- A claim is the contact you make with the insurance company when something has happened. It includes an accurate description of what has happened. A claim is made so that the insurance company can honour its agreement with you.

- An adjuster examines the damage or injury and makes a decision about the amount of money paid out by the insurance company.

- Replacement value is a coverage which will give you the amount of money needed to replace the lost or damaged items at today's prices. There is a higher premium for this type of insurance. Otherwise, there is a cash settlement for the depreciated value of your items. For example, coverage for a ten-year-old TV will not likely get you enough money to buy a new TV.

- An appraisal is a judgement of the value of an item, usually made by an expert.

- Some items, such as expensive jewellery, fur coats, and stamp or coin collections are not covered by general insurance policies and must be appraised and then insured separately.

- A rider, or floater, can be purchased to cover these items which are appraised and must be insured separately. These can be attached to your policy so that it will include all the items you want to insure.

Complaining the Write Way

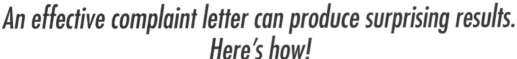

An effective complaint letter can produce surprising results. Here's how!

1 Calm down. Never complain when you're angry. Presume the company will be happy to respond to your complaint. Make sure your complaint is valid — be reasonable in your expectations.

2 Save your receipts, warranties and other relevant information. It helps to include the serial number and a copy of the warranty and receipt when you write to complain. Don't throw any broken product away… the company may want to examine it.

3 Make sure your letter is legible. A typed letter gives a good impression but, if yours is handwritten, make sure it's easy to read.

4 Address your letter to the person in charge. If it's to a major corporation, check your public library for the correct spelling and address. Judge whether your complaint is important enough to write to the President of the company. If someone at a lower level can handle the complaint, indicate you're sending a copy to the President.

5 Establish your relationship with the company. If you are a loyal customer, say so. If it is the first time you patronized the store, then tell them what lead you there in the first place.

6 Clearly state the exact problem. If your complaint is with service, include names, locations and dates. If it is a problem with a product, include all relevant details.

7 Tell them what action you expect! If you want to have the item repaired or replaced, say so. This gives the company an opportunity to please you.

8 Be positive. Write that you hope the problem can be resolved quickly so your confidence in the company can be restored. Include your phone number.

9 Keep a copy of your letter. If you do not receive a reply within 4 to 6 weeks, write again enclosing a copy of your original letter. Let them know you are disappointed. If you didn't write the President before, send him or her the follow-up.

10 If you get results, send a thank you letter. This will encourage the company to keep satisfying its customers and that will benefit everyone who does business with the company in the future.

Rating Our Plastic Pals

by Ron Chalmers

The Journal asked several experts about the best bank card — and discovered that different cards suit different clients.

They all agree that you should clear off your card every month, in full. It's one way to beat the bank — with short-term, interest-free loans.

When you pay no interest, the rate is irrelevant — so these experts carry cards with features other than low interest rates.

"I wouldn't dream of not paying it off," says Maria Holowinsky, vice-president of Adroit Investment Management in Edmonton.

"I looked around, got information on four different cards, then chose a Visa Gold Air Miles card," she says.

In two years, Holowinsky has "earned enough air miles for my husband and me to fly anywhere in North America."

Ian Madsen, who operates a financial advisory service and teaches capital investments at the University of Alberta, carries three cards: a Bank of Montreal MasterCard, Royal Bank Visa card and American Express Gold card.

"I began to use the MasterCard almost exclusively when there used to

be is a small transaction fee on the Visa card," he says.

An annual fee is cheaper for frequent use but a no-fee card is cheaper for a rarely used card. So Madsen carries an annual-fee MasterCard plus a no-fee Visa card "as a backup, be-

> ## "Clear off your card every month, in full. It's one way to beat the bank"

cause some places don't take the MasterCard."

He also has an American Express Gold Card because "when I buy durable items, it extends the warranty by at least a year."

That feature paid off when his com-

puter floppy drive "went kerflooey," Madsen recalls. "It cost $200 to fix, and American Express reimbursed me."

American Express charges interest at up to 14.9 per cent, after a 25-day grace period.

But that's irrelevant to Madsen — because he clears his balance each month: "I try to time my purchases for right after the cutoff date, so I get a free float for about 30 days."

Ernie Zelinski, author of a best-selling book, *The Joy of Not Working*, carries a CIBC Aerogold Visa card. He reckons that the annual fee of $120 is a bargain "because it gives me Air Canada points to travel to speaking engagements, and free collision insurance on car rentals when I'm out of town."

A high fee can be a good investment for an active card user, Zelinski says. "I buy all my home office supplies on my card — and I know a restaurant owner who uses a credit card to buy all the liquor — thousands of dollars a month. He really runs up his points!"

Zelinski hasn't paid a cent of interest in several years — but says he could do better because, in addition to his CIBC Gold Visa card, he holds several cards that he doesn't use.

"Away, way back, I got about four Visa cards and five MasterCards," he recalls.

That was when he'd first discovered the joy of not working — but hadn't yet made it pay.

"I felt I could survive on those cards, if things got bad," he says.

But he prospered in his non-working career, and rarely used those cards.

Now that he won't need cash advances, Zelinski says, "I probably should cancel some of those cards because they have annual fees."

Debra Wooding, branch manager of a CIBC/Wood Gundy investment brokerage in Edmonton, holds two Visa cards — but prefers to use a debit card.

"When I used a Visa card, I would pay it monthly anyway," she says.

"The debit card is so convenient — with no surprises at the end of the month."

Wooding doesn't need the one-month no-interest loans that a credit card can offer. Simplicity is more important because "I've got six children, and I don't always have time to balance my chequebook!"

David Waite, a policy analyst with the Industry Canada consumer affairs office, advises that "if you are running a monthly balance in excess of $400, it really is advantageous to use low-rate cards."

With a large balance, he says, consumers should not be seduced by the reward or incentive programs of high-rate cards. "Incentive schemes are for people who pay off their entire amounts," he says.

FAQ Using Credit Wisely

It is sometimes easy to forget that you have to pay for what you buy. Here are some guidelines for keeping control of your financial affairs and making credit work for you, not against you.

◆ Make a budget for yourself and stick to it. Make sure that you know what is coming in and what is going out. That way you will avoid nasty surprises.

◆ Avoid impulse buying. If you had to pay in cold, hard cash, would you be making this purchase?

◆ Comparison shop as a matter of habit. Never buy anything — and that includes any form of credit — without comparing costs and value.

◆ Always read and understand application forms before you sign them.

◆ Be careful of co-signing a loan or guaranteeing a loan on behalf of others. Remember that you could end up paying off the loan if the borrower cannot handle it. Ask the same questions of the borrower that the lender will. Know the risks involved so that you can make a sensible decision.

◆ Be knowledgeable about the cost of credit. Are you using the right type for your purpose? Are you using a more expensive form of credit than necessary?

◆ Be sensible about the number of credit cards you use. How many do you really need? Are you using them simply because you have them?

◆ Keep track of all your credit purchases. Save the receipts for checking against the monthly statements and for keeping a running total of your obligations. One way you could do this is to get an extra cheque register (the part of the cheque book on which you keep track of deposits and withdrawals.) You could use the "cheques" column for noting credit purchases and the "deposits" column for noting credit payments. The "balance" column could be used for noting how much you owe in total.

◆ Remember, whether you use cash, a cheque, a card or a loan to pay for your purchases, to check out the reputation of the merchant, the store's return policies, the quality of the goods and the product warranty. Using credit to pay for something does not absolve you of your consumer responsibilities.

An (A+) or an (F)?

Every year, people are shelling out interest so they can buy things right away when they don't have the cash.

The A-plus situation is when you're saving and investing a portion of your paycheck. The C-minus situation is when you're spending the whole thing. The F situation is when you're ringing up charges on your credit cards and running up a tab. When that happens you're paying interest to somebody else, usually a credit-card company. Instead of your money making money, the company's money is making money on you.

From Sears to Shell to the banks that sponsor credit cards, companies love it when you buy things with the card and don't pay the entire bill right away. They use their own money to pay your bill. It's a loan from them to you, although you might not see it that way. They charge you a high rate of interest on your unpaid balance. You may be paying them as much as 18 percent, which gives them a better return from your pocket than they could ever expect to get from the stock market. In other words, to a credit-card company, you're a better investment than a stock.

When you buy a $400 TV set on a credit card that charges 18 percent interest, it costs you an extra $72 a year for the loan. And if you pay the minimum amount every month and let this loan drag on, you end up spending $800 for the $400 TV set. Millions of credit-card users haven't figured this out. Every year, people are shelling out interest so they can buy things right away when they don't have the cash.

Instant gratification, it's called, and shoppers pay a high price for it. They read the ads and go into several different stores to find the best deal on a TV set to save themselves a few bucks, then they charge the TV set on a credit card, which may end up costing them an extra few hundred. They do this willingly, without even thinking about it.

In ancient times, forty-five years ago, before Diner's Club came out with the first credit card that could be used in multiple establishments, people actually waited until they had the cash in their hands before they went to the store to buy things. They saved up for their TV sets, appliances, furniture, vacations, and so forth. It might have taken them six months, nine months, a couple of years even, to raise the money to make a purchase, but they never had to pay interest.

Believe it or not, shopping in this primitive way, without instant gratification, was often enjoyable. While you saved up for a TV set, you could sit around the living room and talk about how much fun it would be to have one. Imagining the TV set, or the washing machine, or the new suit of clothes was entertaining in itself.

People felt great pride when they worked hard and made certain sacrifices in order to pay for something all at once. It made them nervous to owe money to the banks, and when they paid off their home mortgages, they had parties and invited all the neighbors to help them celebrate. It wasn't until the 1960s that we got into the habit of using credit cards, and it wasn't until the 1980s that average families were hocked to the limit on mortgages, car loans, home equity loans, and the unpaid balances on their cards.

This is the F situation that many households have gotten themselves into. Instead of their money making money in stocks or in the bank, the bank's money is making money on them. They're paying out hundreds, if not thousands of dollars a year in interest. It's OK to pay interest on a house or an apartment, which will increase in value, but not on cars, appliances, clothes, or TV sets, which are worth less and less as you use them.

Debt is saving in reverse. The more it builds up, the worse off you are.

"Special Offers?"

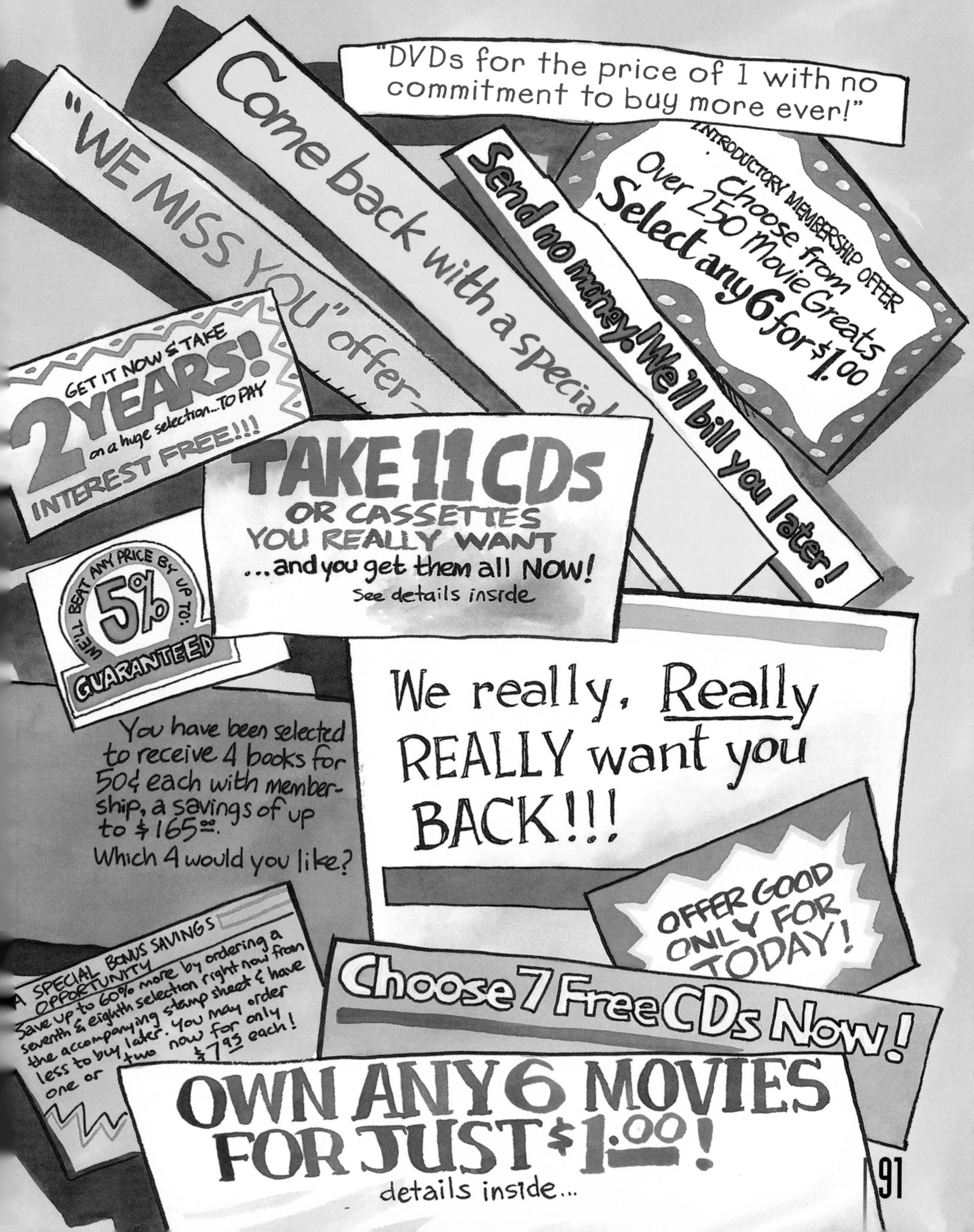

What's Your Comfort Zone?

Every investment has an element of risk; the key is determining how much risk you're willing to assume based on the returns you want to achieve.

Because your risk tolerance is related to your personality, chances are you have a pretty good idea of whether you're an aggressive, adventurous risk-taker or a more conservative, security-oriented person. Here is a brief quiz that can give you an idea of your feelings about risk.

1 If an investment of yours doubled in price five months after you bought it, would you:
- A) Buy more.
- B) Sell half.
- C) Sell all of it.
- D) Do nothing.

2 Making investment decisions is something you find:
- A) Easy.
- B) Enjoyable.
- C) Difficult.
- D) Frightening.

3 If you had a choice, would you rather (choose one item from each of the following two groups):

Group 1
- A) Travel to a foreign country.
- B) Go skiing or sailing.
- C) Enjoy a peaceful week at the cottage.
- D) Work in your garden or golf.
- A) Go to the theatre or museum.

Group 2
- B) Try a new restaurant.
- C) Cook dinner at home.
- D) Read a good book or watch TV.

4 If you held a lottery ticket with a one-in-three chance of winning a $50,000 prize, what would be the least amount of money you would consider selling it for before the drawing?
- A) Wouldn't sell it.
- B) $10,000
- C) $20,000
- D) $30,000

5 If you had to make an important decision that involved your life savings, how would you go about it?
- A) Ask close friends or relatives for their advice, then decide.
- B) Ask a trusted adviser for his or her opinion.
- C) Ask a trusted adviser to make the decision for you.
- D) Develop strategies that reduce your risk of loss.

Scoring:

Give yourself four points for every "A" answer, three points for every "B", two points for every "C", and one point for every "D". Add your total and compare to the chart below.

18-24 points	Aggressive investor, comfortable with risk.
12-18 points	Moderate investor, willing to accept some risk.
6-12 points	Conservative investor, risk averse.

92

It's About Time

- for yourself, for your family, for school,
for leisure time, and for the community.

Feeling stressed? Feel like there is never enough time for all that you have to get done in a day? Do other people seem to get more done?

The truth is that each one of us has 24 hours a day. Take away 8 hours for sleep, a couple of hours for eating, 7 hours for school and there's not much time left, and you probably still have a list of things to do. Is it any wonder that you feel pressured for time when you still need to do at least some of these: a part-time job, transportation time getting to and from school and work, studying, spending time with your boyfriend or girlfriend, keeping up with your friends, spending time with your family, giving something to your community, going to lessons or other classes, playing on a team, shopping, medical and dental appointments, some regular physical activity, watching TV, and time for yourself? And during exams or the holiday season, the pressure can feel even greater.

The trick to getting more out of your day boils down to knowing some organization tricks. The extra benefit of managing your time is that you can reduce the stress in your life that comes from having too many things to do without enough time to do them all.

Usually, the real problem isn't lack of time. Often, it is a lack of organization, not just at school but in all aspects of your life. It's not that you don't care what happens in these parts of your life - you just need to organize yourself a little.

There needs to be a balance in life - for yourself, for your family, for school, for leisure time, and for the community. When you feel out of balance, one out of two things can happen: either you begin to "spin your wheels" - working even harder in one area and letting the other areas of life go so that there is even less satisfaction and more frustration - or you feel so overwhelmed that all effort stops - you just give up trying. Either way, knowing how to organize can help you get your head above water.

Getting organized takes three steps - thinking, planning, and doing:

✦ Take ten minutes each morning - or the night before if that's a better "thinking time" for you - to make a list of all the things you have do in the day and all the things you would like to get done in the day.

✦ Put a star beside those items that *must* be done today. Number them in order of importance if that will help.

✦ Follow your plan in order of importance. If there's time left in your day, do some of the less important things left on your list. It is possible that your plans and opportunities may have to change during the day. Keep in mind that you are trying to organize your life in a disorganized, sometimes chaotic world. What happens to your plans when you have a flat tire, you lose your bus pass, or the boss asks you to work two extra shifts on the weekend? This is where the skill of flexibility comes in. You can change your plans but don't get caught in the trap of ending up doing the less important things while the really important items on your list get lost.

Paper, calendars, or lists cannot organize you. They are helpful tools but the action has to come from you. Only you can decide it is worth the effort to manage your time. No one can manage your time for you (and you would not want anybody to attempt it) but think about how you feel on disorganized days - stressed out, crabby, couldn't care less, or really resenting doing things you have to do?

If you feel out of control now, how do you get started? Nothing makes you feel more like you are in control of your own time than getting one part of your life in control, so finish that essay or clean the garage or pick up your room. Having one thing in your life that you have managed will give you the push to move to the next task.

Managing your time is not an all-or-nothing action. You didn't get disorganized in a day so you will not turn around your life in a day. But little by little, using some of the hints here, and knowing that you can indeed manage your time, over a period of time, you can see great results.

While the Clock's Ticking...

- Take a look at your work habits - you'll be surprised at the ideas you can come up with to save time.

- Do two things at once - like laundry and studying, or travelling and reading.

- File papers when you get them - in your binder, in your book, in a file folder. You won't waste time hunting for them when you need them.

- Keep a pen and paper by the phone so it is easy to take messages

- Keep a calendar handy (taped to the fridge or near the phone) to record your appointments and activities and those of others you live with

- When you are done with something put it away, not just out of sight, but where it belongs. (It will save you dreaded hours of cleaning up when the mess gets out of hand.)

- This also goes for clothing - hang up your coat when you come in, put clothes in the closet, drawers, or the laundry basket - you get the idea.

- You may have to limit the number of things that you do. Learn to say no, especially to those things that don't help you or others in any way.

- Practise your decision-making skills - the better decision-maker you are, the less stress and stalling you will have in your life - both of which eat up time.

FAQ   10 Ways to Protect Your Credit Cards

You may think these ten rules are unnecessary. But if you ignore them, you make it easy for the wrong people to use your cards.

1. Never leave your cards unattended at work. There are more credit card thefts in the workplace than in any other single location.

2. If your credit card is programmed to access an Automated Banking Machine (ABM), protect your Personal Identification Number (PIN) or security code. Don't write it down, memorize it.

3. Don't leave your credit cards in your vehicle. A very high proportion of credit cards are stolen from motor vehicles.

4. Always check your card when returned to you after a purchase. Make sure it is your card.

5. When travelling, carry your cards with you or make sure they are in a secure location.

6. Report lost or stolen cards immediately. Most fraudulent use of cards takes place within days of their being lost or stolen.

7. Sign the back of a new card as soon as you get it. Destroy unwanted cards so no one else can use them.

8. Make a list of all your cards and their numbers. This key information is helpful when reporting lost or stolen cards.

9. Always check your monthly statement. Make sure the charges are yours.

10. Never give your card number over the phone unless you are dealing with a reputable company. The only time you should give it is when you have called to place an order.

Treat your credit cards like cash.